AUSTRALIAN PRAYERS

BRUCE D. PREWER

Chi Rho

Lutheran Publishing House, Adelaide

Copyright © 1983 Lutheran Publishing House.
Except for brief quotations embodied in critical articles
and reviews, this book may not be reproduced in whole
or in part by any means whatever without the prior written
permission of the publishers.

First printing October 1983
Second printing March 1984
Third printing July 1985
Fourth printing May 1986
Fifth printing March 1988
Sixth printing November 1989

National Library of Australia
Cataloguing-in-Publication data

Prewer, Bruce D. (Bruce David), 1931-
    Australian Prayers.

    ISBN 0 85910 258 0

    1. Christian poetry, Australian. I. Title.

A 821'.3

Printed and published by
Lutheran Publishing House
205 Halifax Street, Adelaide, South Australia   89-316

To my oldest friends:
Cliff and Florrie

INTRODUCTION

*'In your prayers do not go babbling on like the heathen,
who imagine that the more they say the more likely they
are to be heard.'*

Having compiled this volume of original prayers, I have become
more aware of the warning which Jesus gave concerning wordy and
repetitious praying.

This collection is gleaned from the last four years of my service as
an ordained minister within the church. About eighty per cent are
prayers which were composed for particular congregations at
particular times. The remainder are some of my own private prayers,
formed during times of meditation, either in the parish setting or
during normal periods of leave.

In my opening sentence above, I used the word 'original'. That is a
foolish word to use. Some wise person has said: 'The art of
originality is forgetting where one first read it.' That must be true in
this case. I am indebted to thousands of people who have shared
their prayers, either in worship beside me, or within books. Also I
have been seeded with the great prayers of the ages, especially
those of the Jewish and Christian traditions. Even beyond that, there
have been times of awareness when I knew my praying has been
God praying through me, as the 'groans of the Spirit' pleaded from
within me. At the end of this complex process, these particular
prayers have emerged with the stamp of my faith and personality on
them. Only in this sense are they original.

They are called 'Australian Prayers'. This is not to claim that they
draw exclusively on the idiom and imagery of Australia. Some are, in
fact, more colourfully Australian than others; but most are simply
the prayers of one Australian praying among other Australians. Do
not expect, or fear, that you will discover kangaroos and banksia
trees waltzing through every page.

There is little that is unique or special about this collection. It is not presented to surprise, shock, or impress. Although unassuming, I hope the prayers avoid both the jargon of academic theology and that cheap, 'folksy' language which has more in common with the prattle of football commentators than holy dialogue. They are simply the record of real praying that happened among God's people; no more than that.

Those confessions, joys, pleadings, and aspirations have now become little symbols printed on paper which have no breath of their own, and may mean little or nothing. This is good. My efforts are reduced to a sane size. Whether they live again is entirely beyond my power. So I am led back to the crux of things: that grace which alone can give new life to one single phrase.

Bruce Prewer,
Pilgrim Church, Adelaide

Easter 1983

CONTENTS

Part IV: GO IN PEACE
Confession and Forgiveness

Part V: GOOD TO BE ALIVE
Thanksgiving and Praise

Part VI: LOVE YOUR NEIGHBOUR
Sharing the Concerns of the Lord

Part VII: AS YOU LOVE YOURSELF
Be with us Lord

Part VIII: FOR SHEPHERDS ONLY
Ministers, Pastors and Priests

Part I

ADVANCE AUSTRALIA
Days, Places, and Moods

Australia Day

God of Australia, you have loved this ancient land
long before human eye explored it. On this Australia Day
we offer mixed feelings of praise and plea for our nation.

We bring you our gratitude
for the diversity and wealth
of this land and its people:
for its weathered old mountains, fertile valleys,
and vast plains;
for its riches of mine and agriculture,
forest, and grazing lands;
for our black people who know and love this continent
with an intimate, profound sensitivity;
for the courage, vision, and sacrifice of the early settlers;
for the diverse races who now call Australia home:
For these and all your gifts
we offer you, O Lord, our joyful, thankful hearts.

We also bring confession
of the evil
which has marred our country
and injured our citizens:
for the rapacious way we have exploited the good earth
for quick monetary gain, with little thought for the future;
for the ugliness we have imposed on places of rare beauty
through our vandalism — both legal and illegal;
for our history of vile inhumanity
toward our black sisters and brothers,
and for the injustices which they still suffer;
for our neglect of minority groups and our continuing
racist intolerance toward some immigrants;
for our blatant selfishness which has helped
create and maintain the caste of the unemployed:

Have mercy upon us, O God.
Bring us to repentance.
Forgive and renew us
with the grace of our Lord Jesus Christ.

God, our God,
take us all and lead our nation
toward the higher destiny
which belongs to the children of God:
through Jesus, our First Citizen and Lord.

Anzac Day

God of the living and the dead,
console and encourage
those for whom this day
is one of profound significance.

Be with the widows,
spinsters, orphans and the totally disabled,
who together with the dear and honoured dead
have sacrificed so much.
By your grace,
work in the hearts and minds of men and women
who today are reliving
the agony, courage, and compassion
of war service.

Help all of us to honour
those who have made so great a sacrifice,
yet save us
from ever glorifying the evil of war.
Enable us to be peacemakers.
Hasten the great day
when nation shall not lift up sword against nation,
neither shall they learn war any more.

This we pray
in the name of the One who sacrificed his all
for the sake of the world:
Jesus Christ, our Redeemer and Lord.

Labour Day

God of the Carpenter,
we thank you for this day
on which we can celebrate
the value of all who labour
in the basic tasks of our community.

For the efforts
of all those who in recent centuries
have fought for the dignity
and rights of all workers:
We thank you, God of the Carpenter.

For the upgrading
of working conditions, safety precautions,
the length of work-hours,
and justified wages:
We thank you, God of the Carpenter.

For the gift of those
who do the dirtiest jobs,
who have the most boring tasks,
or who are still exposed to dangers:
We thank you, God of the Carpenter.

For all whose health has suffered,
For the weary who don't know how to keep going,
and the weak whose strength is failing:
We pray to you, O Lord.

For all who are still exploited,
especially migrants and women;
For those who are victimized by foremen,
and those who must work beside ugly characters:
We pray to you, O Lord.

For those who do work which is degrading,
people who feel compromised and dishonest,
workers who suffer sexual harassment,
those who have no friends among fellow-workers,
and all who have been demoted at work:
We pray to you, O Lord.

For the many who have recently been sacked,
the thousands who have been unemployed for years;
for the families of the unemployed who are suffering,
and those without work who are tempted to turn to crime;
for the young who feel hopeless about the future,
and the middle-aged who feel useless:
We pray to you, O Lord.

Father of Jesus,
God of all workers,
bless your people
and lead us all
to that time when the workers of this world
may be treated
with justice and respect:
through Jesus Christ, the worker from Nazareth.

New Year's Eve

Lord of all our days,
be with us tonight,
when the car horns hoot,
church bells ring,
crowds shout and cheer,
and 'Auld Lang Syne'
is sung at numerous parties.

Let those of us who love you
celebrate with as much joy
but with more purpose than
those who love you not.

Put a new song of faith
on our lips,
and renew the optimism of grace
within our mind and heart:
through Christ our Lord.

    *   *   *

God of the old year
which is passing away,
we commend to your mercy
those who are glad to finish this year.

We lift up before you
those who have critically overworked,
those who had no opportunity to work,
folk whose health has broken up,
or whose career has been shattered;
our neighbours who have tasted grief,
or who have contracted terminal illness;
people who will end this year homeless,
and those who end it in hunger or thirst.

    *   *   *

God of the new year
which is dawning,
we also commend to your mercy
those who enter the new year eagerly.

We hold up before you
all who will take up new work,
or who will retire from work;
all who plan to be married,
or who look forward to parenthood;
the people who will buy their own home,
or who will commence at universities;
those who will come to faith in you,
and all whose faith will grow stronger.

God of the past, present
and the limitless future,
bless all your people,
that, set free from old fears
or shallow optimism,
we may live with the joy
of the children of God.

Loving This Continent

Source of all love and joy,
Father of Jesus and our God,
to you belongs our gratitude.
Your loyalty to us is untiring
and your love is beyond all measure.
We thank you, Lord of Life.

When our continent was being created
you thought of us and provided for us.
When our land's inhabitants
were kangaroo and koala,
jabiru and carrawong,
alligator and yabbie,
you catered for our needs.
We thank you, Lord of Life.

When we inherited this land,
we used it recklessly and selfishly,
but you did not give us up.
Though, like tramps, we wander among our broken promises,
shattered hopes, and empty prayers,
you give us Jesus the Christ,
to seek and save the lost.
We thank you, Lord of Life.

Though Australians become blinded by technology,
misled by opinion-poll morality,
hardened by greed, and captivated by lusts,
through Jesus Christ you still come among us
inviting us to reclaim our destiny
as your very children.
We thank you, Lord of Life.

God of Jesus,
God of the Southern Cross
and of all who read its sign,
make our nation your nation.
Let us live to your glory,
today
and as long as this land shall last.

Wilderness

The wilderness and the dry land shall be glad,
the desert shall rejoice and blossom.
In solitary places praises rise,
when we are glad for the wilderness.

For the Coorong, with its sand dunes,
waterways and pelican,
the Flinders' flocks of emu
among the daisy plains,
the cedars of New England,
the flame tree, and creepers:
We thank you, God of the wilderness.

For Russell Falls and Franklin gorges,
the grandeur of the Inland,
and the mysteries of Ayers Rock,
the jagged peaks of Stirling Ranges
and their slopes spread with flowers:
We thank you, God of the wilderness.

For the velvet woodlands of the Conway
and the fossicking of brush turkeys,
the heathlands of Yanchep
and black swans by the lake,
the volcanic spires of Warrambungle
and the sungolds ablaze:
We thank you, God of the wilderness.

For Lamington Plateau
with its jungle and paddy-melons,
the screech of cockatoos
among the Grampians' buttresses,
the host of ferns, palms, and mosses
in the oasis of Palm Valley:
We thank you, God of the wilderness

For the bliss of being awed by ancient beauty,
for new perspective given to harassed lives,
for the gift of solitude in the presence of the elemental:
We thank you, God of the wilderness.

Murray River Matins

Communing Spirit,
you share with me
the profound loveliness
of this soft, grey morning
in the stillness of the bush
beside this wide water
which reflects
like glazed ceramic
the sentinel river gums.

Early you watched with me
the approach of the faithful old sun,
which from below the wide horizon
threw shafts of salmon light
upon the low cloud banks,
and deftly tinted
the sleepy face of the creek.

Beside me,
yet through me,
you, most intimate Spirit,
have pleasured intensely
in the seried flights of pelicans
returning from a night's fishing,
gliding authoritatively between
an avenue of gum trees
to take their morning rest
among the feathered tribe
which dozes noiselessly
by a sheltered billabong.

Through my ears
you have listened
to the egret's squawk
as it tries out roosting places
on half-submerged bare tree limbs.
You hear the mournful cry
of the ubiquitous black crow,
the chatter of lorikeets,
and, in between these,
the rare sound of silence.

You, Agape Spirit,
have communed with me
on this gentle morning,
infilling my life with something
of your elemental serenity,
awakening an awe which leavens
the supreme contentment of wholeness,
yet leaves me raw
and more exposed
to threats of existence.

Creator Spirit,
like your Jesus
help me increasingly
to trust your serene communion,
and like Jesus,
when it is needed,
to accept the holy way
of the cross which weighs
so painfully on souls
made sensitive to beauty.

Vespers by the Murray River

The winter sun
finds a gap in sombre clouds
through which to project
its last strong strands of golden light
across the wide old river,
and among the piebald
trunks of river gums,
then plays briefly on the face
of distant red-clay cliffs.

Old man Murray
flows by almost imperceptibly,
silently making pilgrimage
toward his destiny
in the Southern Ocean.
No winds disturb his peace;
and so, gently smiling,
he mirrors the evening shapes,
and tempts a redfin
to leap three times
in spasms of joy.

A grey heron,
its yellow legs knee-deep,
wades with ballerina delicacy
along the river's flank.
A pure white egret
patiently stands statuesque,
its perfect reflection
like a Siamese twin
looks up at it from the water.
Then a flotilla of pelicans
glides effortlessly by with the dignity
of stately galleons
from some bygone age.

All is still and gentle
as if all creation shares
with tender empathy
the last whisper
of this dying day.
The lights are low now,
and everything is suspended
as if waiting
for some final word.

Then without warning,
with no introit,
God's cheerful choristers
the kookaburras
dent the evening air
with the joyful vesper
which has been sung
across our motherland
from time immemorial.

And I, a late migrant
to this scheme of things,
feel my spirit leap within me
to share this ancient canticle
of gratitude and joy.

Lord, now let your servant
lie down in peace this night;
and, if it pleases you,
let me wake tomorrow
to the song of your glad choir
among these aged gums,
chanting a jubilant sanctus
for the gift of a new day.

Huon Pine

Lord, how I enjoy
the aroma and feel
of this timber of yours
which spins
on my wood-lathe
like a prayer-wheel.

Here, revealing to me
its texture,
are a thousand years
of growth and setback
in the rain forests
of the Franklin.

Here is the nurture
of a Creator
who is not in a hurry
to achieve
things of rare beauty
and utility.

A millennium of seasons
coded here
in the fine grain:
torrential rains, blankets of snow,
and the energy of the sun
in a thousand Springtimes.

How many times
did this fragment of creation
vibrate with birdsong,
the growl of Tasmanian tiger,
or the chant and dance
of early Aborigines?

What deep secrets
does it hide
as I attempt
to plane and polish it
into new patterns
of beauty?

As I touch this texture,
grant me the sensitivity
to learn from this Huon Pine
yet another parable
of the Creator's
joy and pain.

Canberra

God of the 'City Splendid',
we pray for our Federal Capital of Canberra:

city of superb planning and of high hopes,
city of noble architecture and national treasures,
city of politicians, public servants, and tourists,
of university, Mint, and embassies,
of growing churches, families, and schools;

city of endeavour and much frustration,
of tarnished ideals and crumbling hopes,
of intrigue, rumour, and cynicism,
city of weary public servants,
the coliseum of those hungry for power,
the cemetery of fallen idols
and broken idealists.

In your great wisdom and mercy, Lord,
forgive and bless your city of Canberra.

Song of the Jarrah

Master,
incomparable woodturner,
you take tough jarrah
    like me,
    and from it
fashion things more beautiful
    than eye has seen
    or ear heard.

Some days
you uncover in me
    a grain-pattern
    fine and elegant
which I never knew
    I possessed.

Sometimes
you work patiently
    through sapholes
    knots, or rogue grain,
spinning contours of grace
    in spite of all.

Carpenter,
irrepressible craftsman,
you even became jarrah
    in the lathe
    in order to share
    the pain of the mis-shapen,
    the joy of the new-shaped,
and the love song
    of jarrah's Creator.

Ancient Gumtrees

Lord, your ancient, noble red gums
    scattered across the grass lands
    of southern plain and valleys,
never fail to move me,
awakening a mood
of admiration, awe,
and meditation.

Their weathered, warped limbs,
    gnarled and distorted
    like the arthritic limbs,
    hands and fingers,
    of one most dear to me,
insist on reaching
out and up
in some defiant ballet
of divine celebration.

Immense trunks,
    bent in a long-past
    sapling-youth
    by prevailing winds,
    and scarred from storms
    which centuries ago
    tore out limbs,
invite me to touch
and gently feel the texture,
or rest my cheek
in love.

Fed by massive, mis-shapen roots
    which, before my life began,
    had already explored
    the ground of their being
    and found it sufficient,
these old folk, Lord,
of your other kingdom,
share with me
the secret of grace.

God of Winter

God of winter,
we praise you:
God of soaking rains,
of hail and snow, wind and storm,
of torrents surging down creek beds,
streams filling reservoirs,
and tanks full and running over.

God of brisk winter mornings,
of frosted paddocks under moonlight,
of warm socks, coats, and gloves,
heaters, radiators, and glowing fires.

God of birds singing eagerly
when the gentle sun breaks through clouds,
of mallee trees tipped with new growth,
and wattles budding, eager for spring.

God of stark hillsides,
clothed for a season in soft green,
and of moist cultivated wheatfields,
where tractors work long into night.

God of little children splashing in puddles,
sailing make-believe boats in flooded gutters,
of raincoats, and umbrellas, and gum-boots,
and the scent of hot soup from the kitchen.

God of winter, glorious winter,
the unpopular, slandered season,
yet one filled with renewed hope
for farms, town, and city.

God of life-sustaining winter,
author of re-creation and providence
renewing the roots of life,
God of glorious winter,
blessed is your name
in all the earth!

An Evening in Autumn

Blessed be your name, O most blessed giver of seasons.
This autumn evening is your gift;
   the gentle air caresses our faces,
   the scent of soil after rain
   is fragrant in our nostrils,
   the body relaxes,
   and the mind absorbs the quiet of dusk.
The meal time is over,
   children have ceased their games and gone inside,
   and the birds have ended their songs —
except for the evening call
of a lone wagtail from a jacaranda tree.
Above and beyond our planet,
the velvet flanks of space
   begin to glisten with the light of stars
supported by a thin crescent of light from a young moon.

This evening, Lord,
our praise rises as simply and sweetly
as the call of that lone wagtail.

'It is good to give thanks to the Lord,
to sing songs of your love, Most loving One!
To affirm your presence in the morning,
and at evening to sing of your love,
to pluck the strings of the guitar,
to give melody to the flute
and make harmony on the harp.
Your deeds, O Lord, fill me with gladness;
your gifts move me to songs of joy.'
Hallelujah!

Signs of Grace in Springtime

Our Father in Jesus and our God,
earth and sky,
sunshine and rain,
tree and flower,
speak to us of your creative power.
Lord, open our eyes to see your beauty.

The sheep on the plains,
the cattle on the hills,
the fish of the sea,
and the birds of the air,
tell of your bountiful providence.
Lord, open our hearts to experience your goodness.

The jacaranda bursts into flower
with a robe of royal beauty —
a symbol of Christ our Redeemer,
of glory he alone is fit to wear.
Lord, you are the King of love, and we are your people.

The lush greening of the vines
reminds us of Jesus, the True Vine,
in whom we must abide
if we are to bear fruit.
Lord, you are the Vine, and we are the branches.

The crimson bottlebrush
witnesses to the blood of the cross,
the cost of our salvation,
and the wonder of forgiveness.
*Lord, your mercy makes all things new;
we open our lives to your grace.*

The singing of the birds
at dawn and dusk
awaken within us the melodies of
faith, hope, and love,
stirring a hunger for the world-wide harmony
and peace which you have promised.
Lord, we thank you,
we trust you,
we love you,
we praise you,
and we worship your name,
world without end.

Without You, Life Is Desert

God, how we need your help!
Without you, life is like the Stony Desert;
with you, life is like the Channel Country
after abundant rains.

If we have become bare and unfruitful,
like a neglected paddock,
be to us as a plough in hard ground.

If we have wandered in waste places,
becoming lost and blinded in sandstorms,
lead us to some quiet, verdant gully,
where there is living water to refresh us,
soft ferns to caress our tiredness away,
and sweet rest on the mossy bank
of your grace, mercy, and peace.

God, how we need your help!
If we are to live fruitfully,
and love our fellows with a love like yours,
we need you every hour!

Lament for My People

Lord, my people have become mopokes,
enjoying the darkness,
but blind in the light.
Where is Australia going, Lord?
Is there any hope for this people
that I dearly love?

What will become of a people
whose gambling bill far outstrips
all pensions to the needy —
who feed rump steak to greyhounds,
and do not notice unemployed citizens
sorting through rubbish bins?

Is there any future for a people
who spend a thousand times more
on assorted pet foods
than they give to the starving
people in our cruel world?

What will become of a society
where married couples
prefer pets and yearly travel
to the joys and disciplines
of family love?

Can we survive as a nation
when, before every election,
our first question is:
'What is in it for me?'

Lord, have mercy.
Christ, have mercy.
Lord, have mercy.
And save us all.

Speak your word of judgment and mercy
to me — and to all my fellow-Australians.
For my people are your people, Lord,
and you understand them
and love them more profoundly
than I ever can.
Lord, when we burrow like wombats to evade you,
deal with us with strong discipline;
make us face the truth,
and live by the light that shines
in Jesus Christ our Lord.

As Raucous as the Wattle Bird

As the raucous cry of the wattle bird
sounds from among fresh gum blossom,
so must my discordant praise sound
in your ears,
my love, my life, my Lord!

Yet you know that my prayer is true,
that my songs of joy are the sweetest melodies
that my heart can compose.

If there is singing among the holy angels
when lost coins and sheep are found,
and when lost children return home,

there is also great joy
among the lost things of this earth
when we, who are found, discover
that you have made a home with us,

and that heaven and earth are becoming one
through Jesus Christ our Lord.

Jubilate Deo!
My love, my life, my Lord!

Such a Strange Mixture

I'm such a strange mixture, Lord;
something greater than human wisdom
    is needed to sort me out
    and make me whole.

Some days I soar like an eagle
    over the peaks of the Great Divide;
Yet on other days I'm like a cockroach
    hiding in dark places.

Sometimes, like a surfer at Coolangatta,
    I truly enjoy riding life's rough waves;
But at other times I just sit and complain,
    allowing the surf to break over me,
    filling my eyes with grit
    and my soul with self-pity.

There are special moments of prayer
    when I beg you to take me hiking
    among the mountain-places of the Spirit —
Followed by pessimistic moods
    when my bleating prayers
    rise no higher than ant hills.

Lord, you have searched me and known me.
You know the strange mixture
    that hides behind my public face.
Take me in hand.
Be to me not the God I want,
    But the God I need.

Part II
WHEN IT'S IN SEASON
Events in the Church Calendar

Preparation

This is the season of His coming;
Night is far gone, the day is at hand.

It is time to wake from sleep;
*For the Son of Man comes at an hour
we do not expect.*

His coming is the advent of saving love.
Come, Lord Jesus.

His coming is good news for the poor,
freedom for captives, sight for the blind,
liberty for the oppressed,
and acceptance for the unacceptable.
Come, Lord Jesus.

Then shall the lame man leap like the hart,
and the tongue of the dumb sing for joy.
O come, O come, Immanuel.

Wake Us from Slumber and Apathy

Advent God,
awaken us from our slumber,
shock us out of our apathy.

Come to us
    like the thunder of the surf
    pounding Bell's Beach,
    like the mighty roar of the wind
    surging through blue gum forests.

Come to us
  with whatever shock
  or discipline is needed
  to awaken drowsy disciples.

For the night is far spent,
the dawn is at hand,
and now is our salvation nearer
than when we first believed.

Come, O come, Immanuel,
save your Australian people;
confront us afresh
until all hearts are full
of the Word made flesh.

Advent God,
we praise you!
Glory to the One who comes
in the name of the Lord!
Hallelujah!

Come, Advent God

Come, Advent God,
and complete the special work of love
which you began in Jesus of Nazareth.

Many are cast down with spiritual needs,
thirsting for the peace of your forgiveness
and the warmth of your healing love.
Come to them with the grace they desperately need.
At evening or midnight, morning or midday,
Come, Lord Jesus.

Many are in despair through physical hardship,
seeking relief from their burdens
and hope in the midst of their cares.
Come to them with the help they desperately need.
At evening or midnight, morning or midday,
Come, Lord Jesus.

Many have minds and souls filled with hatred,
lives shackled by prejudice and terrible obsession
in Northern Ireland, the Middle East, Africa,
South America, Asia, and in our own Australia.
Come to them with the conversion they so desperately need.
At evening or midnight, morning or midday,
Come, Lord Jesus.

Your church in all the world also needs saving
from everything that threatens its mission.
Where it is persecuted, keep it faithful.
Where it persecutes, rebuke it.
Where it is seduced by affluence, shake it to its foundations.
Where it is self-satisfied, thoroughly unsettle it.
Where it is weak, poor, and meek, bless it with your joy, peace
and strength.
At evening or midnight, morning or midday,
Come, Lord Jesus.

Come, Advent God,
and complete your work in Jesus Christ,
through whom we offer these prayers.

Christmas Confession

If we have arrived at a time in our lives
when the Christmas story no longer
excites or renews us:
Have mercy upon us, O God.

If, in the midst of the riches of the Gospel
of Jesus Christ, we live like paupers:
Have mercy upon us, O God.

If the life of Jesus fails to challenge us,
or his death and resurrection cease to comfort us:
Have mercy upon us, O God.

If, in the face of the world's great need,
we hoard the Gospel like misers:
Have mercy upon us, O God.

(Silent meditation)

So that we may be forgiven and renewed:
Restore to us the joy of salvation.

So that we may be a loving community:
Restore to us the joy of salvation.

So that we may clothe our good intentions
with the garments of action:
*Restore to us the joy of your salvation,
through Jesus Christ our Lord.*

Emmanuel

God, in your grace and mercy,
you gave us your Son to be our Emmanuel;
give us a renewal of faith and life at this Christmas time,
and save us from our myths and evasions.

When we trivialize the Christmas Gospel:
Lord, have mercy.
When we talk of peace and goodwill,
with so little of it in our own lives:
Lord, have mercy.
So that we may not only sing carols and light candles,
but also serve the Christ
and allow the light to shine in and through us:
Lord, have mercy.

We thank you,
most generous God,
for all the peace and joy
which you give us.
We thank you
for sins forgiven,
hope renewed,
relationships repaired,
faith rekindled,
for your great love in Jesus Christ
established once again in our lives.

Jesus, our Emmanuel,
God with us,
we worship you
and joyfully offer the praise
of heart, voice, mind, and strength.

Remembering the Needy at Christmas

Lord, on this wonderful day we pause
to remember the needy people of this world
whom Jesus came to save:
May the light of his star touch every dark place.

As we meet in fellowship and goodwill,
we pray for the end of war and terrorism
in your torn world, especially ...
As we eat, drink, and are merry,
we pray for the hungry, homeless, and diseased:
Bring them your compassion and justice, Lord.

As we enjoy being relaxed and happy today,
we remember the sick,
the lonely, the frightened,
the anxious and the sorrowing:
Bring them your comfort and peace, Lord.

As we prepare to leave this place of prayer
to go our separate ways,
we remember those friends and loved ones
who are not with us this Christmas:
Give them the assurance of your presence, Lord.

As we pass other churches,
we remember other denominations,
praying especially for those
we fail to understand or appreciate:
Fill them with Christmas joy and praise, Lord.

O Word made flesh,
give us the will and capacity
to embody our prayers
in compassionate and courageous deeds:
Fill us with the joy of service.

God in the highest, worthy of glory,
hasten the day
when the song of the angels shall find perfect fulfilment:
In the name of your incarnate Son, Jesus.

Contradictions

God of vast generosity,
   your love planned the birth of the Baby
   who is born to save his people from their sins:

We confess to you and to each other,
   that, in this world of contradictions,
   we stand in need of your saving.

Forgive us
   if in the Christmas season we have used holy words
   in a shallow way,
   if we have conducted hollow celebrations,
   if we have given gifts only to those who give to us.

Forgive us
   if we have feasted without thanksgiving,
   caroled without joy,
   greeted without caring,
   and prayed without love.

May the living Word which has come to us —
   Emmanuel who is with us,
   Elder Brother who is one of us —
save us from our sins,
quieten us with his peace,
and fill us with his Spirit.

We delight to call his name Jesus,
for he is saving us from our sins.

Searching and Finding

Most loving God,
   who put it into the mind of the Wise Men
   to search for Jesus,
please give to us the wisdom to seek and to find.

When we become proud and stubborn,
give us the wisdom to find our humble Lord,
born in a stable.

When we become bewildered and lost in life's rush,
give us the wisdom to find ourselves
in the light that streams from Bethlehem.

When we become selfish and covetous,
cluttering our lives with possessions,
give us the wisdom to find that the best joy lies
in offering our treasures to Christ.

When we become depressed by our human failures and sin,
give us the wisdom to find the divine compassion and mercy,
the forgiveness which Jesus came to bring,
enabling us to name him Saviour from personal experience.

God of the Wise Men and our God,
put into our minds the wisdom
   to follow the star which leads us to Jesus Christ,
and to follow him, come what may,
   till our travelling days are done
and you call us home.

On Transfiguration Day

God of the transfigured Christ,
in your mercy transfigure us
and the whole world,
till the glory of Christ is seen
in the most unexpected places.

Transfigure our schools,
universities, medical schools,
and military colleges.

Transfigure our hospital wards,
our foster homes,
and our funeral parlours.

Transfigure our politics,
business and industry,
our laws and lawcourts.

Transfigure our friendships,
marriages, neighbourhood,
and all places of work.

Transfigure our charities,
overseas aid programs,
our refugee procedures and hostels.

Transfigure the church universal,
the churches of ...
and this congregation at ...,
as we meet for worship and service.

And in your boundless grace, O God,
transfigure our own
personal faith, hope, and love.

Lord of the mountain and plain,
of vision and sacrifice,
let us live in the light
and glory of your love
today and for ever:
through Jesus Christ our Lord.

Lent

O come, let us return unto the Lord:
For he will have mercy and abundantly pardon.
The Kingdom of heaven is at hand;
repent and believe the Gospel:
His will is our peace.
His discipline is our hope.
His service is perfect freedom.
In his presence is fullness of joy.

You cannot live by bread alone:
Lord, have mercy.
You shall not test the Lord your God:
Christ, have mercy.
You shall worship the Lord God,
and him only shall you serve:
Lord, have mercy.

O God, we are so immersed in the materialism of our age
that we find it hard to recognize our sins:
Open our eyes to see ourselves as you see us.
Expose the secret gods within us,
pinpoint the deceits that blur our perception,
unmask the poverty of our souls,
expose our greed, arrogance, or apathy,
save us from our love of things and use of persons,
deliver us from morbid guilt, cheap discipleship,
and sentimental religion:
through Jesus Christ who suffered and died for us.

Palm Sunday

Most loving God,
we confess that we are in danger
of making Palm Sunday a ceremony
rather than allowing it
to be an event in our lives.
Lord, have mercy:
Lord, have mercy.

If we sing our hosannas
within the safety of the church,
but rarely in public life,
Christ, have mercy:
Christ, have mercy.

So that our timidity may be transformed into courage,
and our indifference turned into costly love,
Lord, have mercy:
Lord, have mercy.

(Silent meditation)

Lord, have mercy upon us;
Christ, have mercy upon us,
Lord, have mercy upon us.

We thank you, O God, for Christ Jesus:
the word of forgiveness, the gospel of hope,
and the grace of new creation:
Hosanna! Blessed be the one who comes
in the name of the Lord.

We are grateful for the assurance
that Christ Jesus came into the world to save sinners:
Hosanna! Blessed be the one who comes
in the name of the Lord.
Hosanna in the highest!

He Who Comes

Hosanna! Blessed be the King who comes in the name of the Lord:
Hosanna in the highest!
If we should hold our peace, the very stones would shout aloud:
Hosanna in the highest!

God of the King
   who humbly rides on a donkey,
we who are conceited about our image and status,
   need your salvation:
Come, Lord, save us.
God of the pilgrims
   who publicly confessed their enthusiasm for Jesus,
we, who are embarrassed by public displays of faith,
   need your salvation:
Come, Lord, save us.
God of the hesitant
   who watched the holy procession,
   but were in two minds about joining it,
we, who often falter in our convictions,
   need your salvation:
Come, Lord, save us.

Gracious God, we thank you
for the experience of forgiveness
and the sense of your presence:
We praise your grace in Jesus Christ,
who makes disciples out of sinners,
and creates new life in tired or barren lives.

Hosanna! Blessed be the mercy
which comes in the name of the Lord:
Hosanna in the highest!

The Suffering Servant

O Lord, our Lord,
we have heard the most unlikely story;
we have seen your saving power in a weak Man.

He grew up quietly like a lonely plant,
    rooted in arid ground.
There was nothing to make one notice him,
    no good looks to impress the crowd.
His people despised and rejected him;
    a suffering, pathetic, neglected creature,
from him most turned their faces,
    reckoning him as useless.

Yet, unlike anyone else, he bore our lot,
    and carried the full ballast of our sorrows;
but we carried on as if he deserved his fate,
    sentenced to misery by God.
The wounds he bore were for our faults,
    the crown he wore was for our violations;
He suffered shame to bring us peace,
    tasted pain that we might be healed.

We are as stupid as sheep,
    wandering and lost;
but in and through this Man
    you have carried our shame.
His rights were openly violated
    yet he took it without complaint —
like a ewe before drunk shearers,
    as a lamb led to slaughter.

From the land of the living he was cut off;
    by our sins he was struck down.
Though he was never a violent man,
    nor ever spoke a treacherous word,
he died between criminals,
    and was buried in a borrowed grave.

Yet You did not forsake this bruised servant;
   you made his death the unique death,
and did the most unexpected thing:
   He rose to life again!
After the agony came light;
   after disgrace came vindication:
victory for himself and for others,
   banishing the burden of human disgrace.

Therefore this weak Man is for ever strong;
   His is the only, truly successful life.
He willingly staked his existence on you,
   and allowed himself to seem useless.
But, in fact, he bore our uselessness,
   and removed all charges against us.
His incomparable love-offering
   has become our true peace.

Behold The Man

Holy God,
this is the day
we most love,
yet hold in most awe.
We behold the Man,
and tremble.

O God,
as Jesus is lifted up,
our faith must either
be renewed or lost.
We see Him
and recognize
the kind of person
we want, yet are afraid, to be.

Behold the Man,
despised
outcast
accursed —
quite dispensable
when the powerful
snap their fingers
or rattle their money-bags.

God, we confess that
the things we deeply fear
meet us at this execution.
It is a nightmare,
from which we wish
to hide our faces:
from the One who seems abandoned
by earth and heaven.

This Golgotha is the place
where our smooth, sensible ideas of
success
power
wisdom
faith
and divine love
are shattered by a hammer beat.

Either we must abandon
this world's wisdom
and begin again,
or we must abandon
You, God.
Here at this Cross
our faith either rises
or falls.

Lord we believe,
Help us in our unbelief.

Ecce Homo!*
Ecce Deus!**

* Behold the man!   ** Behold your God!

Good Friday Intercessions

God of the crucified Jesus, we pray:

For the church:
that we may be courageous in carrying the cross,
compassionate in forgiving our enemies:
and willing to use our resources
in love for all for whom Jesus died.

For Australia:
that our Australian nation may be both just and generous:
and experience the grace that comes
from losing life and finding it.

For the suffering:
that sick, hungry, or suffering people
may know your love and receive your help
which they need physically, mentally, or spiritually:
In the fellowship of Christ's sufferings,
may they know there is a God who understands.

For our families and friends:
that, according to their individual needs,
your divine strength may be experienced in human weakness:
and that hopes that have been buried
may germinate and grow,
and be ready for a resurrection.

For each of us here:
that we may be lifted above anxieties, guilt,
bewilderment, pain, or fear,
and, by the mercy of the Jesus
who bore our sorrows and carried our shame,
find peace at the foot of the holy cross.
Blessed be your name,
God of the Crucified,
Friend of all the needy and forsaken.

Easter

God of the risen Christ and our God,
we rejoice in your resurrection power,
which is fully ours in Jesus Christ,
and we pray that you will keep us alert
to the sufferings, needs, or duties
that burden many people this Easter.

Keep us prayerfully aware of those
for whom this Easter is one of misery and loneliness:
   those who are separated from loved ones,
   immigrants who are lonely in a strange environment,
   alcoholics and other addicts
   for whom no day is ever a holiday,
   homeless young people,
   unwanted old people,
   and the inmates of our prisons:
Living Lord, help them to know your love in the message of Easter,
and to rejoice in the gift of life in Christ.

Keep us aware of those
for whom this Easter time is one of tragedy:
   especially the victims of road accidents,
   their family and friends,
   those who are seriously injured,
   those who are fighting for very life,
   and those who are weeping for the dead:
Living Lord, help them to know your love in the message of Easter,
and to rejoice in the gift of life in Christ.

Keep us aware, O God, also of those
who must work while most of
us are holidaying:
  policemen and prison warders,
  transport workers, and entertainers,
  ministers and priests,
  ambulance men and nurses,
  cooks and nightwatchmen,
  and all those who are busier than usual
  in catering for guests:
Living Lord, help them to know your love in the message of Easter,
and to rejoice in the gift of life in Christ.

God of Easter, keep each of us aware of our own needs,
and of the vast resources for our growth in faith, hope, and love,
which are available to us this day of resurrection:
through Jesus Christ our Lord.

Easter Mercies

Christ is risen:
He is risen indeed.
The King of glory is among us:
He entered the gates of our humanity.
Who is the King of glory?
The Lord of the stable and the cross,
He is the King of glory!

Who is this King of glory?
Jesus, the Word made flesh,
He is the King of glory!
He came to dwell among us,
and we saw his glory,
such glory as befits the Father's true Son,
full of grace and truth.
Christ is risen for us:
He is risen indeed! Hallelujah!

God of the risen Lord Jesus,
as we glory in your power
which raised up your Son,
give us more faith and hope;
help us to know
the availability of your power
in our weak lives.

When we despise and discourage ourselves,
Lord, have mercy:
Lord, have mercy.
When we despise and discourage others,
Christ, have mercy:
Christ, have mercy.
When we despise the grace of forgiveness,
maintaining the spirit of bondage,
Lord, have mercy:
Lord, have mercy.

(Silent meditation)

Hear the Gospel:
Christ is risen!
He is risen indeed!
Who dares condemn us?
Christ has died for us,
Christ is risen for us,
Christ intercedes for us.
What shall separate us
from the love of Christ?
Nothing,
Nothing today or tomorrow,
Nothing in life or death,
Shall separate us from God's love
in Christ Jesus our Lord.

The Right-hand Man

God of the humble and homeless,
    the poor and the persecuted,
thank you for exalting Christ Jesus
    and giving him a name
above all other names.

Today we rejoice
that he who was the meekest and weakest
    of all earth's children
is at your right hand.

Now we know
that the homeless Son of man
    is more truly at home
than anyone else on earth.

Today we rejoice
that he who was the poor teacher,
    who begged for a cup of water,
    and slept on the wild heath,
shows us our way to glory.

With gratitude we sing
    of the Man on a cross
who's now the exalted First-born
    of a new, everlasting race.

God of the defeated and the lonely,
    the despised and the hungry,
the misjudged and the imprisoned,
    the suffering and the dying,
we rejoice with great joy,
    praising his name,
and adoring your love!

City Pentecost

Through skyscraper canyons
    you come, Holy Spirit,
  down lanes and arcades
    you come:
  From the north, from the south,
  from within and without,
    like wind
    like wind
  the roar of Pure Wind,
  you come
  sweeping through
  to renew.

In houses of parliament
    you come, Holy Spirit,
  into lawmakers' chambers
    you come.
  From above, from below,
  from ally and foe,
    as truth
    as truth
  the roar of Pure Truth
  you come
  sweeping through
  to renew.

Through grand gothic arches
    you come, Holy Spirit,
  to choir and high altar
    you come.
  From the west, from the east,
  from the font and the feast,
    like fire
    like fire
  the roar of Pure Fire
  you come
  sweeping through
  to renew.

Pentecost Confession

If we have followed other spirits,
rather than the Spirit of Jesus,
Lord, have mercy:
Lord, have mercy.

If we have refused to give full rein
to the Spirit in our deeds and words,
Christ, have mercy:
Christ, have mercy.

So that we may be filled
with the loving fruits of the Spirit,
Lord, have mercy:
Lord, have mercy.

(Silent meditation)

The Spirit you have received is not a spirit of fear,
leading you back into slavery,
but the Spirit of adoption,
through which you call God
'Father, my very own Father'.

Spirit

Spirit of God, active in creation:
Spirit of love,
Spirit of Jesus, one with our Saviour:
Spirit of love,
Spirit of life, present in the Church:
Spirit of love.

We rejoice in your presence
around us and in us,
through the precious Gospel of Christ,
like wind on our faces
and breath in our lungs:
Presence of joy.

We rejoice in your power
to give new birth and new life,
like fire, warmth and radiance,
like life in dormant daffodils
bursting forth in spring:
Presence of hope.

We rejoice in your accepting us,
ceaselessly seeking us,
freely treasuring us,
with love older than mountains
or the distant stars,
new every morning:
Presence of grace.

Creator Spirit:
Spirit of love,
Life-giving Spirit:
Spirit of love,
Nurturing Spirit:
Spirit of love,
We bless you for your mercy,
love you and adore you.
Blessed be your name
of love for ever and ever.

Holy Spirit, Help Us

Holy Spirit, you make all things new;
renew us in will and deed
to work together with you.

That all people, who today are shivering
with an icy loneliness at the core of their being,
may let go, and let God fill them with his warmth:
Spirit, hear us; Spirit, help us.

That Christians may be more willing to trust the Spirit
to fill and renew their lives and relationships:
Spirit, hear us; Spirit, help us.

That disabled people, the sick, and the disadvantaged
may find the Spirit with them and in them,
giving new courage and serenity:
Spirit, hear us; Spirit, help us.

That bitter people, disillusioned people,
and the angry ones who cause war or terrorism,
may find an inner healing of the Spirit
that will lead to peace and reconciliation:
Spirit, hear us; Spirit, help us.

That those who cause or tolerate injustice and inhumanity
may be brought to repentance
and find the way of the compassionate Spirit:
Spirit, hear us; Spirit, help us.

Spirit of God,
Gift of Pentecost,
remake us in the likeness of Christ,
that we may live to your glory,
from here to eternity.

Trinity

When we lose faith in the goodness of creation,
and in the father-like love of our Creator:
Lord, have mercy.

When we lose faith in Jesus as the true reflection
of your suffering, death-conquering, redeeming love:
Christ, have mercy.
When we lose faith in your Spirit's presence among us,
working through your implanted Word:
Lord, have mercy.

Most loving God,
for the Word of mercy made flesh in Jesus Christ,
unmistakable and uncompromising in strong compassion:
we give you thanks.
For every word of love and forgiveness,
in individual people, in fellowship, and in prayer and worship:
we give you thanks.
For that insight or understanding within us,
that allows us to accept forgiveness
and to live with the joy of the freedom of God:
we give you thanks,
through Jesus Christ our Lord.

All Souls

Author of life abundant and eternal,
we thank you for the cloud of witnesses
　　who make the mysterious heaven
　　a home for our hearts.
Before you, we remember
　　those faces we love
　　and those spirits we treasure.

At radiant dawn
　　and in the quiet of dusk:
we remember them.
Under summer skies
　　with the farmlands shimmering:
we remember them.
Through winter's storms
　　mid frost and snow:
we remember them.
At the return of spring
　　with wattles clad in gold:
we remember them.
At birthdays and family celebrations,
　　and in the festivals of the church:
we remember them.
When Christmas arrives
　　with its carols and candles:
we remember them.
In the house of God
　　as we sing and pray;
in the trumpets of the dawn
　　on Easter Day;
in the Bread we break
and the Cup we take
　　with eucharistic joy:
we remember them.

Our Paradox King

God of our Paradox King,
God of Bethlehem's son
and Nazareth's man,
Father of our Brother and Lord,
Friend of the poor:
Your name we adore,
Now and evermore.

King of the blind and the lame
and the leper with no name,
Jesus, Brother and Lord:
Your Spirit we love,
Your name we praise.

King of wild flowers and lilies,
ravens and sparrows,
Jesus, Brother and Lord:
Your Spirit we love,
Your name we praise.

King of lonely and outcast men,
and much-abased women,
Jesus, Brother and Lord:
Your Spirit we love,
Your name we praise.

King of all who are betrayed,
and those falsely tried,
Jesus, Brother and Lord:
Your Spirit we love,
Your name we praise.

King of the criminal dying,
and the forsaken crying,
Jesus, Brother and Lord:
Your Spirit we love,
your name we praise.

King of empty tombs and graves,
and limitless life,
Jesus, Brother and Lord:
Your Spirit we love,
Your name we praise.

God of the Paradox King,
love in the present,
love all transcendent,
Father of our Brother and Lord:
Your name we adore
now and evermore.

Part III
SMALL IS BEAUTIFUL
Collects on Various Themes

On Fieldlarks' Wings

As the fieldlark
rises at daybreak
to offer its praise
high above wheatfields,
trees, and farmhouses:

So may we,
in this hour of awakening,
let our gratitude ascend to you,
O Lord Most High.

On the Rays of the Morning

God of the inner light,
come to us
   on the golden rays of the morning,
   warming moods that are frosty,
   enlightening minds that are gloomy;
and, as the sun swings higher,
so may our lives rise to you
   in the active praise of this day's duties:
through Jesus, our risen Light.

Trusting New Life

Spirit of new life,
grant unto us this day
   the grace to recognize new life
   breaking through
   in unlikely events;
and, in so recognizing it,
   to be ready to trust it
   and delight in it:
through Jesus Christ our Lord.

Twentieth-Century Saints

Most loving God,
hope and joy of all who are
pure,
humble,
poor,
hungry,
merciful,
and ready to suffer for righteousness' sake:
Keep us faithful in the love of Jesus,
that we may be his twentieth-century saints and disciples:
In his loving, saving name.

As Eagle and Dolphin

O God, you are my God:
early will I seek you,
my soul thirsts for you,
my flesh longs for you.
As the eagle belongs to the air,
and the dolphin belongs to the sea,
so we belong to you,
O God, my God.

Daybreak

Most loving God,
we who worship in the early hours of this day
pray for the grace
to accept all duties and pleasures
as a gift from you,
and by the help of your Spirit
to allow all things
to work together for good:
through Jesus Christ our Lord.

Touch and Heal Us

Most loving God,
  in whom we live and move
  and have our being,
give us new awareness of your presence.

Touch our minds,
  that we may know you
  in the word of Scripture
  and in the living Word, Jesus Christ.
Touch our ears,
  that we may hear you in music and song.
Touch our eyes,
  that we may remember you
  in the signs of cross and candlelight.
Touch our hearts,
  that we may love you
  with a love that sweeps through us
  like a great tide.

Living, loving Spirit of God,
touch us with the spirit
of love, joy, and praise.

Like a Plover

God, tender and strong,
  as the plover defends her young
  against their enemies,
so defend me
  against those anxieties and nameless fears
  which are my enemies.
Save me in the hour of trial,
  and deliver me from evil.
Under your wings
  let me shelter
until faith and courage return:
for your love's sake.

For Lightweights

Most wonderful God,
great strength is yours
to exert at every moment:
  look gently upon our frailty.
And, although we weigh no more
than a grain of sand or a drop of dew,
  fill us with your Spirit
that we may become weighty
in matters of grace, mercy, and peace:
through Jesus Christ our Lord.

Divine Generosity

Generous God,
Your open-handedness goes far beyond what we deserve,
and higher than our noblest aspirations.

We do not ask for more blessings,
but for the ability
to recognize, enjoy, and extol
the ones that are ours for the taking:
through Jesus Christ our Lord.

Morning

Creating God,
   as the curtain of night is drawn back,
   and the golden robes of the day
   arrive over sea and mountain,
expel from our minds all sour thoughts,
that we may greet this new day as a gift
   fresh from the hands of creation,
   and filled with hope, and bright with gladness,
and glorify the One who makes all things new:
through Jesus Christ our Lord.

The Word and the Babble

Loving God,
give us a lively and sensitive mind
that we may hear your Word
above the babble of human words;
and, so hearing,
may follow every suggestion
you make to us this day:
through Jesus Christ our Lord.

Unspeakable Joys

Loving God,
you have knit together your people
in one communion and community
within the mystical body of Jesus Christ.
Give us grace
so to follow your saints
in all faithful living,
that we may participate in the unspeakable joys
which you have prepared for all who love you:
through Jesus Christ our Lord.

Needed Gifts

Give us, O God,
diligence to seek you,
wisdom to recognize you,
purity of heart to know you,
and a faith
that may love and embrace you:
through Jesus Christ our Lord.

Listen to Our Brother

Almighty God,
    you are the source of all life.
Help us, your children, to listen
to our Elder Brother,
Jesus the Christ,
    that in him we may discover
    the fullness of life,
    and be delivered from all false goals
    and all crippling fears:
through Jesus Christ our Lord.

Reedwarbler

Lord of peace,
at this evening hour
under the open skies,
create within my soul
a vesper as pure
as this melody
which rises near the riverbank
from the throat
of your little reedwarbler.

God of the Evening

Now that dusk is near —
   with parrots in the gum trees
   lessening their chatter,
   with the distant roar of cars
   fading to a mere murmur —
may I hear
the 'voice of the One
who walks in the garden
in the cool of the evening',
   and, in hearing that voice,
find a little of the Eden-peace
which some day will be perfected.
This I pray
in the name of him
who was once mistaken for a gardener.

Joy on Grey Days

Joyful Spirit, Holy God,
   on grey days which dawn
   but slowly and sullenly,
still give us the grace
   to sing with the magpie,
   and laugh with the kookaburra:
through Jesus Christ our Lord.

Bonuses

God of grace and God of glory,
you have invited us to share
the bonuses and burdens of your kingdom
with Jesus
our Elder Brother;
grant that we may continue to accept your offer,
and bring forth deeds of grace
after the example of our Christ:
in whose name we pray.

When Honour Departs

O Lord, our Lord,
   as times arrive when it is appropriate for us
   to relinquish tasks and positions
   which have brought pleasure and honour to us,
help us to do so
with the dignity and beauty
of the poplar trees in autumn,
   so that, in both gaining and losing,
   we may live to your glory:
through Jesus Christ our Lord.

A Quiet Spirit

Teach us, good Lord,
to pray as we should,
so that we, who so often babble
like the heathen,
may be released from our much asking,
and brought to rest our lives
in the hands of the Father
who knows our needs before we ask him.

Victorious

O God,
You raised up your true Son
   to crush evil and give us abundant life.
Grant that, filled with this Gospel,
   we may seek the company of Christ Jesus,
so that in his nurturing friendship
   we also may become victors over all evil,
and begin now the promised life of the ages.
This we pray in his name.

New Year's Eve: Endings and Beginnings

God of things old and things new,
    of precious memories and exciting hopes,
help us to complete this old phase of our life,
and to begin the new
    in the peace, joy, and courage to be,
    which is your personal gift
    to all who will receive it:
through Christ Jesus,
the hope of yesterday,
today, and for ever.

This New Day

Most loving God,
you have given us this new day
in which to serve you
and to delight in you.

By your Spirit help us to do so,
not as slaves,
but as your precious children,
called to be the sisters and brothers
of our Lord Jesus Christ,
in whose name we gather this morning.

Incarnation

Almighty God,
you have wonderfully created us,
and even more wonderfully saved us
through the holy incarnation.
Grant, we pray,
that, as Jesus completely shared our nature,
we may increasingly share his spirit
and live to your glory,
and thus inherit the life abundant
which you have prepared for us
in and through Jesus Christ our Lord.

Hearing the Angels' Song

Most wonderful God,
   whose glory angels sang
   when Christ was born,
help us who hear the good news
truly to know it,
and, in knowing it, to believe,
and, in believing, to obey —
   that we may rejoice in your peace,
   and live to love one another
   even as you have loved us:
through Jesus Christ our Lord.

Faith

Living God,
   faith is your gift to us.
We thank you for the faith we have,
and pray you to enlarge it,
   so that, by faith,
   our hope in you will be more radiant,
   and our love purer, stronger,
   and more courageous:
through Jesus Christ our Lord.

Christ the King

God,
we thank you for Jesus,
   our Prince of peace
   and our King of love.
Blessed by his love,
and freed by his forgiveness,
may we follow that royal way
which exalts
   forgiveness,
   mercy,
   truth,
   generosity,
   courage,
   compassion,
   and faithfulness.
This we ask for his name's sake.

Advent

O God,
you make us glad each year
when we remember
the birth of Jesus.

Grant that we may
joyfully receive him as Redeemer,
serve him as Lord,
and love him as Brother and Friend,
now and for ever.

Partners in Love

God of new creation,
we thank you that ultimately
  there is only one energy
that links all together:
  the vigour of your love.
Grant that this day
  we may be partners with you in love,
and so bring out into the open
  the glory which so often lies hidden:
through Jesus Christ our Lord.

Good Shepherd

Most loving God,
in Jesus, who gave his life for the sheep,
you have opened up to us
the way of limitless life.

Help us to know Jesus our Good Shepherd,
  that we may be able to recognize his voice
  among the many voices that call to us;
and, knowing his voice,
may we have the courage
  to follow wherever he leads us,
that our lives may be opened
to the limitless life
which you offer to all your children.

This we pray,
in the name of our Good Shepherd,
Christ Jesus our Brother and Lord.

Part IV

GO IN PEACE
Confession and Forgiveness

Shame and Glory

Most loving God,
we admit to you and to each other
that we are beings in whom shame and glory
are strangely mixed.
We are creatures of wisdom and folly,
   trust and anxiety, success and failure,
   truth and deceit, love and apathy.
We need you, yet we evade you —
   to believe, yet we doubt,
   to praise, yet dishonour,
   to love, yet resent.
God of the new creation and our God,
we wish to be made whole
   in thought, word, and deed.
We seek of you today the gifts of Jesus:
   forgiveness, renewal,
   self-acceptance, self-understanding,
and the courage to be
the sisters and brothers of Christ.

To Be More Loving

God of grace, God of glory,
   we turn to you
   for the word of forgiveness and new life.

When we criticize others
for the same weakness that lies hidden in us:
Save us, good Lord.
When we take a legalistic attitude
rather than the difficult stance of love:
Save us, good Lord.
So that we may live the law of love
in all its discipline and freedom:
Save us, good Lord.

Loving God,
we thank you that through Christ Jesus
you have saved us,
you are saving us,
and you will save us.

Losing Faith

All knowledge is yours, O God,
   and you know us better
   than we know ourselves.

If we lose faith in ourselves as your children:
Forgive and restore us.
If we lose faith in your pervasive goodness and mercy:
Forgive and restore us.
If we lose faith in the Word that, where sin abounds,
grace much more abounds:
Forgive and restore us.

All knowledge is yours, O God,
   and all love comes from you.
In your own wise way and at your time,
transform us into the people
   you would have us be:
through Jesus Christ our Lord.

When We Fail to Love

Jesus said: Everything in the law and the prophets hangs on two things:
You shall love the Lord your God,
with all your heart and soul,
and mind and strength;
and you shall love your neighbour as yourself.

I confess to you, most loving God,
and to you, my Christian family,
that, although I honour Jesus Christ,
I fall far short of his example.

I am a disciple of little faith.
My loyalty wavers, my vision is limited;
my prayers are selfish, and my sacrifice is rare.
I confess that my love for God and my neighbour too readily grows cold.

But, despite our sin, we know
our God is merciful.
I pray for the forgiveness that renovated Peter,
the compassion that healed Magdalene,
the grace that accepted Thomas,
and the love that wiped away the tears of Mary.

Who shall rescue us from this body of defeat and death?
God alone, through Jesus Christ our Lord!

Lord, we hear your voice:
Child, your sins are forgiven you;
go in peace.
Thank you, God of faithfulness,
love, and new life.

Failure to Love

Living God,
you raised Jesus from death
to be the power of saving love
in our midst.

We confess our failure
   to entertain and trust his love.
We have not loved you, God,
   with his fervent love.
We have not loved others
   with his class of love.
We have not even loved ourselves enough
   to cherish and nurture our own lives
   in the ways of Christ Jesus.

As a result, our characters are stunted,
   our lives mis-shapen,
   and too often, fruitless.

Have mercy on us, we pray.
Break down all the barriers
   which we erect against your love.
Enter the dark or dusty places of our being,
   purifying and enlightening us.

Restore to us
   the joy of your salvation,
and renew a right spirit within us.
May Jesus Christ grow larger
   in all our activities:
In his gracious saving name.

Faith and Works

If we have become obsessed with the needs of our own soul,
and neglected the deeds of faith:
Forgive us, merciful Lord.

If we have become so preoccupied with good works
that we have neglected your nurturing grace for our spirit:
Forgive us, merciful Lord.

That we may be possessed
by the lovely, balanced spirit of Jesus our Christ,
bringing health to our prayers and deeds:
Take us over, merciful Lord.

We thank you for this moment of honesty and insight,
and for the assurance of your saving grace.
*Blessed be your lovely and loving name
for ever.*

To Know Ourselves

Most merciful God,
help us this morning to trust your grace —
    more than misers do richness,
    or politicians power.

That we may know ourselves through and through,
yet not be afraid:
Lord, have mercy.

That we may frankly face
our foolishness and our shortcomings,
yet not be despairing:
Christ, have mercy.

That we may be aware of
our gifts, virtues, and strengths,
and not hide them under a fake humility:
Lord, have mercy.

Where sin abounds,
grace much more abounds:
The law came through Moses,
but grace and truth
through Jesus Christ our Lord.

Hurry and Worry

God of eternity, creator of time,
giver of life and love,
rescue us from those pressures
which throw us off balance.

If today we have been in too much of a hurry
to realize that it is good to be alive:
Lord, have mercy.

If we live too close to the news headlines,
and not close enough to the eternal verities:
Christ, have mercy.

If we become so worried
that we forget that your grace is sufficient for us:
Lord, have mercy.

Timeless God, steadfast in love,
generous and patient with all your creatures:
*let the peace of our Lord, Jesus the Christ,
garrison our lives this day.*

Lost in the Traffic

Because we become confused in the traffic of life,
and easily lose our way:
Lord, have mercy.
Because we often seem unable to transform wrong turnings
into opportunities for grace and growth:
Lord, have mercy.
So that we may see more clearly, act more creatively,
and move forward with the courage of our convictions:
Lord, have mercy.

Most merciful God,
who alone can help us find our true direction,
deliver us from confusion,
   defend us in temptation,
strengthen us in weakness,
   and keep us on the road
which Jesus has taken.

Double Standards

Because we get angry about trivial matters,
but remain apathetic in the midst of grave injustices:
Lord, have mercy.
Because we take a rigid stance when criticizing others,
yet plead special consideration and understanding for ourselves:
Christ, have mercy.
Because we readily legalize the old commandments,
and sentimentalize the new commandment:
Lord, have mercy.

God of Jesus, help us
to turn from our double standards,
to accept your acceptance,
to discard our guilt and anxiety,
to make amends where it is possible,
and then to get on with business of living in the Spirit.
In the name of our Lord, we pray.

Judge Not

Because we indulge in the destructive sin
of dividing people into rigid categories of good and bad:
Lord, have mercy.
Because we attempt to bolster our own ego
by playing at being judge:
Christ, have mercy.
So that we may encourage and assist
people who despise themselves to stand up tall:
Lord, have mercy.
God with us,
Spirit of truth,
you are present everywhere,
    filling all things;
treasury of love,
    the reservoir of life,
please dwell in us.
Remove all ugliness,
and foster health in every part:
through Jesus Christ our Lord.

For Recovery of Joy and Liberty

Because we too readily become discouraged
and half-hearted about our discipleship:
Lord, have mercy.
Because we allow our values and attitudes
to be distorted by the pressures of society:
Christ, have mercy.
So that we may recover our joy in the Gospel
and our liberty in loving service:
Lord, have mercy.

Lord, we pray that your grace
may always precede and follow us,
and enable us continually to give ourselves
to the good works of your new world:
through Jesus Christ our Lord.

Bring Us to Our Senses

Loving God,
because we carry burdens on our own shoulders
that we could have shared with you:
Lord, have mercy, and bring us to our senses.
Because we have listened to many conflicting voices in society,
and failed to take time to listen to your still, small voice:
Christ, have mercy, and bring us to our senses.
So that we may be freed from guilt and needless anxiety,
and experience the peace of forgiveness and renewal:
Lord, have mercy, and bring us to our senses.

All-pervasive God,
   in whom we live and move and have our being,
so guide us in the ways of mercy and truth,
and rule us by your Spirit,
   that, in all the cares and occupations of life,
we may keep cool heads and loving hearts,
   as we walk the way
of our Lord and Saviour, Jesus Christ.

Part V

GOOD TO BE ALIVE
Thanksgiving and Praise

Full of Grace and Truth

In the thick of a crowd —
   some hearing,
   some fearing,
weary woman forces through,
   touches his hem,
   is whole again:
Glory to the Son,
full of grace and truth.

When the sun is setting —
   the crowds now gone,
   he, now alone,
climbs the near mountain,
   finds the grace
   of a solitary place:
Glory to the Son,
full of grace and truth.

At the dawn of a day —
   he is beholding
   wild heath unfolding,
Solomon far outstripped,
   bellbirds ringing,
   magpies singing:
Glory to the Son,
full of grace and truth.

In a proud man's house —
   tired, reclining,
   harlot arriving,
washes his feet with tears,
   her shame released,
   goes in his peace:
Glory to the Son,
full of grace and truth.

In an olive grove lonely —
  vigil keeping,
  courage seeking
to drink the bitter cup:
  sweat-blood falling,
  agony appalling:
Glory to the Son,
full of grace and truth.

Nailed to rough wood —
  life-blood spending,
  heavens unbending
at the cry of him forsaken,
  gasping, crying,
  alone in dying:
Glory to the Son,
full of grace and truth.

Beside waters at dawn —
  fishermen trawling,
  Stranger calling:
'Throw wide the nets',
  breakfast prepared
  served by the Lord:
Glory to the Son,
full of grace and truth.
Glory, glory,
Glory to the Son,
Firstborn of the children of God.

Gloria In Excelsis

Yours is the glory:
  Light in the word
  Word in the silence
  Warmth in the cold
  Life in the cell
  Love at the threshold.
Yours is the glory
Beginning and end.

Yours is the glory:
  Light over Eden
  Dust standing tall
  Praying and crying
  Loving and losing
  Laughing and sighing.
Yours is the glory
Beginning and end.

Yours is the glory:
  Light over Bethlehem
  Laughter in Nazareth
  Sunshine through Galilee
  Gloom in Gethsemane
  Cloud over Calvary.
Yours is the glory
Beginning and end.

Yours is the glory:
  Light from a tomb
  Love new arising
  Greeting and mending
  Renewing indwelling
  Trusting and sending.
Yours is the glory
Beginning and end.

Yours is the glory:
　Light in community
　People enlivened
　Liberated and caring
　Body of Jesus
　Impudent and daring.
Yours is the glory
Beginning and end.

The Name: Jesus

For the name of Jesus, Saviour, and the Word made flesh:
Blessed be the Lord God.

That we are forgiven:
Blessed be the Lord God.

That we are rescued and accepted by love divine:
Blessed be the Lord God.

That his name is Emmanuel, God with us:
Blessed be the Lord God.

That we are adopted into the family of God,
and are indeed sisters and brothers of Jesus:
Blessed be the Lord God.

That nothing in life or death,
earth or heaven, past, present or future,
can separate us from the love of Christ:
Blessed be the Lord God,
For he has visited and redeemed his people!

Endless Love

We thank you, God,
through our Lord Jesus Christ,
for the assurance of forgiveness
and the promise of renewal.
Your everlasting name
is mercy and love.
At morning, noon, and night,
You are mercy and love.

You are compassion;
Your love never ends.
You are our hope;
Your love never ends.
You are our inspiration;
Your love never ends.
You are true liberty;
Your love never ends.
You are joy and peace;
Your love never ends.

At morning, noon, and night,
you are mercy and love.
Holy is your name
above all names;
and, by your grace,
holy is our gratitude:
through Jesus Christ,
our Saviour and our Brother.

Focus

God of light,
   Father of the True-man,
   when we commune with him
   we find the clear focus
   for every scattered ray of light ,
   that has warmed our day
   or cheered our night.

Encountering him,
   all fond theories
   and all other options —
   no matter how brave
   or seductive to reason —
   become mere chatter
   and games of evasion.

Through him alone
   you offer that sheer grace
   which can create much
   out of very little —
   or out of nothing,
   in our darkest hours,
   make everything.

Your relentless Christ
   leaves nothing unchallenged,
   nothing unused;
   every seed of faith
   is nurtured and warmed,
   while every vagrant aim
   becomes transformed.

Though he lives large,
   Man ahead of man,
   he never engulfs us
   nor deserts us in the ruck;
   the irreversible cross
   and discarded tomb
   allow no loss.

Baptized by the Morning

Risen Lord Jesus,
as the rising sun
baptizes trees and shrubs
in rippling light,
let me be baptized
by your resurrection light.

May I
trust in you above all else,
hope in you above all other goals,
seek you in all things,
find you in every situation,
meet you among all people,
know you over everything —

And love you with adoration
beyond
beyond
beyond all telling.

Great Thanksgiving

Lift up your hearts:
We lift them to the Lord.

Let us give thanks to the Lord our God:
It is right to give him thanks and praise.

For this lovely planet, earth;
for its beauty and fertility;
for the human family with its many races and faces;
and for Your utter faithfulness to us
in spite of our rebellion and sin:
In the name of the Father, most generous Creator, we thank you.

For the deeds and words of the prophets and saints;
for the Word made flesh in Jesus our Brother
who lived among us, suffered and died for us,
and rose with abundant life:
In the name of the Son, most gracious Redeemer, we thank you.

For your renewing presence, creating the Church
and inspiring deeds of justice and love:
In the name of the Spirit, most Holy Comforter, we thank you.

With angels and archangels,
and with all the company of heaven,
we proclaim your great and glorious name,
for ever praising you and singing:
Holy, holy, holy Lord, God of power and might,
heaven and earth are full of your glory.
Hosanna in the highest.

Blessed is he who comes in the name of the Lord.
Hosanna in the highest.

Thanksgiving for Light

Most wonderful God, we thank you for the gift of light:
For its power to cheer us, enliven us, encourage and guard us.
For the merry old sun, rising over our hills and calling us to a new day:
For moonlight and starlight, stirring a sense of wonder
and serenity within us.

For street light, car light, traffic light, protecting
and guiding us:
For the beauty of city lights viewed from the hills.
For the beauty of affection lighting the faces of those
who love us:
For the light of human compassion in hospitals, nursing
homes, and counselling agencies.

For the supreme light of divine love
in the face of the Man of Nazareth:
For the radiance of Christ's goodness, grace, and
self-sacrifice.
For his light in his church, exposing, challenging, and
showing us the way to new creation:
For his radiance in our individual lives, uncovering,
rebuking, forgiving, renewing, and guiding us.
Most wonderful God, we praise you
for the Light of the world:
Most merciful God, we praise you
for the Sun that is never eclipsed!
God of God, Light of Light,
Glory be to you now and for ever.

Evening Prayer

The busy day now takes its rest,
as mother evening enfolds us in embrace.
The distant stars and galaxies signal
messages about a Creator so vast
that our minds stagger
and our hearts are filled
with loving awe.

O Lord, our Lord,
glorious is your name in all the universe.
What are earth's children
that you notice us?
And what is the mystery of divine grace
that you love us?
You give us faith to trust you,
even though we cannot see you.
You touch our minds with fingers of light,
and our hearts with forgiveness and peace.

As the evening moves on,
we go to rest
able to sleep the sleep of children
who know that, in life or death,
we are surrounded by love eternal.

O Lord, our Lord, glorious is your name
on earth and in the heavens!

Good to be Alive!

God, our Father in Christ,
it is good to be alive,
to share life with each other
in your wonderful creation:
We are most grateful,
and we thank you, Lord.

You have given us the opportunity
to see the spring flowers,
to watch trees in the wind,
to inhale the fragrance of the season,
and to feel the warmth of the air:
We are most grateful,
and we thank you, Lord.

God, it is good to rest in the evening,
and rise in the morning,
to walk upon this good earth,
to hear your whisper in many places,
and to sing your praise with many friends:
We are most grateful,
and we thank you, Lord.

Lord, like a generous friend
you share the whole world with us,
and you fill our cup to overflowing
with the wine of gladness:
We are most grateful,
and we thank you, Lord.

We want to sing, dance, and pray,
in gratitude for every good thing in your creation!
Especially we want to embrace and express your Spirit;
the Spirit that filled our Lord Jesus to overflowing,
the Spirit of mercy, forgiveness, courage, and new life;
the Spirit of love, and laughter, and peace:
We are most grateful,
and we thank you, Lord.

For your presence with us, around us, beneath us,
within us, behind us, and in front of us:
we, your children, are most grateful,
and we thank you, through Jesus Christ our Lord.

For Faith

Most wonderful God,
we thank you for the faith we have;
help us to trust you more.

We thank you
for all that keeps us believing
    that our lives have meaning,
that our coming and going
    are noticed by our Heavenly Father,
that disappointment, sickness, fear, or death
    does not cut us off from you,
that always there shines
    the light of Jesus Christ
to sparkle in our happiness
    or lighten our darkest hours.

We thank you
for the meaning given to us
    by those who love and cherish us;
for the purpose injected into our lives
    by wise friends and counsellors;
for the fellowship of the Church
and the wisdom of the Holy Bible;
    for the love which your Spirit spreads in our hearts.

We thank you
    for our faith in grace and mercy,
    for the call to repentance,
    the forgiveness of sins,
    the constant miracle of a new start —
all made possible
through what you have done,
and are still doing,
through Jesus, our Brother and Lord.

Most wonderful God,
    may an awareness of your divine love
soak through our every artery and vein,
    every nerve, tissue, and muscle,
through every cell of our brain
    and into the mysterious depths of our soul,
till we respond to you
    with every fibre of our being,
and worship you as you deserve:
through Jesus Christ our Lord.

Good Morning

The dew is a thousand eyes
shining across the parkland.

The silk sculpture of the spider
glistens between rails on the fence.

May everybody outdoors this morning,
from the grandmother collecting milk
to the pyjama-clad child on her trike,
    know that life is good,
    the world is beautiful,
    and that You, Creating Spirit,
    are the Highest Good
    and the Most Beautiful!

Good morning,
O Lord,
Good morning!
Glorious is your name
in all the earth.

Special People

We thank you, O God,
for those people who are channels of your love in our lives:
For those who gave us birth,
and, in the weakness of our infancy,
sheltered, nurtured, and treasured us.

For those who taught us to walk,
to talk and to explore tastes, smells, sounds,
and to experience the warmth
of belonging and embracing.

For those who overlooked our faults
and affirmed our strengths,
and the friends young and old
who share our tears and laughter.

We thank you, Lord,
for the people of strong faith
who stretch our minds and enlarge our capacity
to explore and understand your ways.

For those at every stage of our journey
who teach us trust by trusting us,
who enable us to love others
through the experience of being loved.

We thank you for those very sincere people
who have demonstrated the joys and disciplines
of the kingdom of God,
and especially people who taught us to love you,
rather than to be afraid of you.

God of love, God of Jesus,
for these healing experiences of growth and loving,
and for the knowledge that the best is yet to come,
we praise your holy name:
through Jesus Christ our Lord.

A Child's Gratitude

Dear God,
thank you for letting us live
in your wonderful world!

Thank you for
kookaburra and kangaroo,
koala, emu, parrot, possum,
pelican, brolga, and willy wagtail.

Thank you for our pets:
dogs which run to meet us,
the purring of cats,
the singing of canaries,
and the chatter of budgies.

Thank you, God,
for playmates and schoolmates,
penfriends and church friends,
for the kindness of grandparents,
and the care of mother and father.

Thank you, God,
for all good and beautiful things —
and most of all for Jesus
who brings us your great love for us.

Springtime

Most wonderful God,
all your works praise you,
speaking your glory and singing of your grace:
We thank you, Lord.

For the changing mood of nature,
with the promise of a springtime soon to come
and its signs around us:
We thank you, Lord.

For the wattle putting on its golden robe,
the almond blossom purer than snow,
for the white and pink heath in our hills,
for the growing cheerfulness of birds,
singing their songs at dusk and dawn:
We thank you, Lord.

For the renewing pleasures of human love and friendship,
for friends returning from holidays,
for loved ones close to us,
for letters and cards telling of births,
engagements, weddings, and travel:
We thank you, Lord.

For the deep-down springtimes of heart, mind, and soul,
spiritual insights and new joys,
music, art, prayers, books — and the Holy Bible,
and the uplift of a congregation
singing the new songs of faith:
We thank you, Lord.

For the call to new life of Jesus Christ,
the word that gives challenge and encouragement,
the life that awakens the hopes of the world:
We thank you, Lord.

For the ministry of the Holy Spirit right now,
for the divine love at hand
to forgive and renew like living water,
washing away all that is sordid, guilty, and unlovely,
and allowing the new growth of faith and hope to take over:
We give you thanks and praise,
through Jesus Christ our Lord.

For All His Mercies

For the forgiveness of sins
and the renewal of our self-respect —
give thanks to the Lord,
for he is good:
His mercy endures for ever.

For the ministries of the church
in pastoral care, music,
fellowship, service,
education, prayer,
and the challenge of the living Word —
give thanks to the Lord,
for he is good:
His mercy endures for ever.

For daily life,
with its sunshine and rain,
toil and rest,
food and drink,
love and friendship,
tears and laughter —
give thanks to the Lord,
for he is good:
His mercy endures for ever.

For people who love us enough
to put up with us when we are irritable,
thoughtless, selfish, or unkind —
give thanks to the Lord,
for he is good:
His mercy endures for ever.

For the generous bonus
of knowing the love of God
through Jesus Christ,
that in him we live and move
and have our being —
give thanks to the Lord,
for he is good:
His mercy endures for ever.

Part VI

LOVE YOUR NEIGHBOUR
Sharing the Concerns of the Lord

Inasmuch

Lord most merciful,
you meet us in unexpected places and people.
Help us to be alert to meet you,
That you may heal our wounds,
and make us ready to serve you
in the needs of our neighbours.

Where you are hungry and homeless,
help us to be your loving people,
giving food and shelter:
Help us to be alert to meet you.

Where you are imprisoned or oppressed,
help us to be your liberated people,
giving comfort and help:
Help us to be alert to meet you.

Where you are anxious and despairing,
help us to be your concerned people,
sharing hope and encouragement:
Help us to be alert to meet you.

Where you are sick and dying,
help us to be your consoling people,
standing at your side with comfort and a steadying hand:
Help us to be alert to meet you.

Where you are the victim of violence and warfare,
help us to be your peace-filled people,
active in peacemaking and rich in love.
Help us to be alert to meet you.

And to you alone,
ever-living and ever-loving God,
be the praise of our lips
and the service of our lives,
now and for ever.

Where People Live

Where people live with a bitterness of spirit
which poisons and distresses those around them:
Your kingdom come.

Where people live greedily, without gratitude or grace,
keeping a ruthless eye on the possessions of others:
Your kingdom come.

Where folk resort to violence, rape, terrorism, and warfare,
spreading suffering and accelerating hatreds:
Your kingdom come.

Where people suffer disease, handicap, or savage injustice,
without any faith to support them:
Lord, your kingdom come.

Where communities of mixed races
ache with ugly fears and hatreds,
and the grief which follows repression or violence:
Lord, your kingdom come.

For all who sit with the dying,
make funeral arrangements,
or spend tonight sleepless and grieving,
we pray for the gift of divine comfort.

Lord, your kingdom come,
Your will be done
on earth as it is in heaven,
through Jesus Christ our Lord.

Transforming Misfortunes

Most loving God,
in this cynical world help your people
to prove the hopefulness of existence
by turning negative situations into positive ones:
When we are weak, then we are strong.

Help folk to transform
disappointments into new courage,
or pain into greater caring and sharing:
When we are weak, then we are strong.

Help people to use sickness
for increased sensitivity toward all who suffer or grieve,
and to make us treasure our neighbours all the more:
When we are weak, then we are strong.

Help us all to use reproach for honest self-assessment,
and abuse for better understanding of others who are abused:
When we are weak, then we are strong.

Help the lost to use their dismay
to spur them into finding themselves and their true destiny:
When we are weak, then we are strong.

Help each of us here
to find your word though prayers seem unanswered,
and to hear your call in difficult opportunities:
*We can do all things through Christ
who strengthens us.*

Our City

God of Jesus,
we pray this morning for our fair city of ..., your gift to us.

We think of its character
noble in history,
proud of its founders,
but often blind
to the source of their inspiration.

Lord, we are proud of its cultures, but troubled about its soul,
proud of its festivals, but troubled about its unemployment.
For some it is the scene of their success-story;
for others it is the place of poverty,
injustice, neglect, and despair.

Merciful God,
help this our city, and your city.

We pray for the city council,
the police, the magistrates,
social workers, town planners,
schools, hospitals, transport authorities,
the directors of big business-houses,
and all the community organizations
who work for the health of our city.

King of the 'City Splendid',
help us to make our city
closer to the city
you would have it be,
through your life-changing love in Jesus Christ our Lord.

Strengthen Our Resolve

Let us pray for others.

   For the church:
that it may be released from all adultery
with materialistic culture and power;
God, hear our prayer:
Lord, strengthen our resolve.

   For our Australian nation:
that political idols may be broken,
and covetousness lose its power over us;
God, hear our prayer:
Lord, strengthen our resolve.

   For the nations of the world:
that false witness by the manipulators may be exposed,
stealing from the weak by the strong be outlawed,
and killing by suppression, starvation, terrorism, or war
be banished for ever;
God, hear our prayer:
Lord, strengthen our resolve.
In the name of Jesus Christ, we pray.

Our Black People

God of our ancient people,
Lord of all tribes,
show those of us who are
more-recent arrivals
in this great south land
how best we can allow Aborigines
to recover their dignity,
and to make their rich contribution
to the well-being of our growing nation.

Thank you for those in government,
and in the church community,
who are really listening
and responding with true wisdom
to their needs and cries.
Thank you for some land rights restored,
for much progress among tribal groups,
for emerging aboriginal poets,
priests, ministers, and managers.

We pray with anguished soul
for the descendants of tribes
disinherited long ago,
for those broken spirits
who gather without aim or hope,
in parks and lanes of cities and towns.
Lord, we feel incapable of discovering
how we can help —
except perhaps to admit to them
that we are burdened to belong
to the race that helped corrupt them.

Lord, hear our cry;
Many of us long to undo
the many wrongs,
as far as that is possible.
But how do we start, Lord?
Where do we start?
Lord, hear our cry!

Planting True Vines

Make our lives, good Lord,
through Jesus our true Vine,
living branches of faith, hope, and love
so that the existence of others may be enriched
and our own lives grow mature with the fruits of Jesus Christ.

For our brothers and sisters
in all their diverse needs,
we pray.

Where people have forgotten how to laugh,
touch them with your joy.
Where they have lost the art of mercy,
graft compassion and forgiveness within them.
Where they neglect to share bread, medicine, trust and friendship,
stir new growth of love within them.

Lord,
our true Vine,
abide in us
that we may abide in you.

Let your presence support the weak,
encourage the sick,
comfort the dying,
guide the confused,
heal the broken-hearted,
soften the hard heart,
and sweeten the bitter spirit.

Let the harvest of our prayers,
be in your time
and in your way, most loving Lord.

For Church and World

Prayer for a Civic Service

In faith, hope and love, let us seek God's blessing on his world and his Church.

Let us pray:
For the church of Jesus Christ in all its branches, in all the world,
for the churches of this nation, this State and this city, enabling
the community of faith to embody the words and deeds of Christ Jesus:
Lord, hear our humble prayer.
For the head of our Commonwealth, your servant Elizabeth our Queen,
and for all governors, governments, councils, and courts under her,
that we may be led in the ways of those who thirst for righteousness
and hunger for peace:
Lord, hear our humble prayer.
For all nations, both our allies and our enemies, that there may be
an end to all injustice, poverty, persecution, and especially for a
just reconciliation between warring factions;
Lord, hear our humble prayer.
For those among our family or neighbours, colleagues or friends, who
are at present living through difficult days of sickness, sorrow, injury,
injustice, anxiety or bitterness, that they may discover the loving
resources of the Holy Spirit:
Lord, hear our humble prayer.
For each person in this congregation today, with personal worry,
heartache, pain or distress, and especially for anyone who feels that they
are at the end of their tether, that these be given recovery of courage
and peace of mind:
Lord, hear our humble prayer.
Most loving God, source of all grace, light, and peace, restore to all
people the joy and health of your salvation, through Jesus Christ our
Lord.

For Those who Hunger

God of Jesus, God of us all,
Only true and everlasting friend,
inspire us to pray and act with the compassion of Jesus Christ.

God, at this moment there are people who hunger for food,
    for a crust of bread, a piece of fish,
    or even the scraps in our garbage bins.
Please feed them:
Lord, hear our prayer, and make us your answer to prayer.

There are some people who hunger for liberty,
    to go as they please,
    to stay on at home or visit friends,
    to worship without hindrance,
    to vote for whom they please,
    to see the end of police, compounds, and prisons,
    to be reunited with those they love dearly.
Please give them liberty:
Lord, hear our prayer, and make us your answer to prayer.

And there are some who hunger to be useful,
    to share what wisdom they have learnt from life,
    to listen to a neighbour's worries,
    to work beside a weary friend,
    to be of use to their family, country or church —
    to be of use to you;
    but bad health,
    or shyness and timidity,
    or unsightly physical deformity,
    or the frailty of old age,
    or sorrow over old sins,
    holds them back and makes them useless.
Please show them how they can still be useful:
Lord, hear our prayer, and make us your answer to prayer.

Loving Father, there are some who hunger for your grace,
  who look for faith,
  who search for your meaning and your name,
  who look for someone whom they can trust,
  and hunger for something worth worshipping.
Please satisfy their hunger with the bread of life:
Lord, hear our prayer, and make us your answer to prayer.

And to you, dear Lord,
Father and Provider,
Christ and Saviour,
Holy Spirit and Friend,
be honour and glory,
worship and praise,
from now to eternity.

The Way of Truth

A Prayer of Young People

Spirit of God,
you are the Spirit of Truth;
lead me into all truth.

While I am growing in body
and enlarging the capacity of my mind,
enable me to grow more Christlike,
as a person of honesty
with deep respect for truth.

Increase my ability to separate
facts from fiction,
honest opinion from advertisement,
friendship from manipulation,
faith from superstition,
love from possessiveness.

Save me from simple trust in
all that newspapers print,
the fantasy world of *Cleo* and *Playboy,*
the gossip that is whispered to me,
the painted public face
and scripted words of TV stars,
or opinions which I'm not prepared
to test with people I trust.

Spirit of Truth,
lead me through the maze
of modern morals,
different religions,
society's many pressures,
and the selfishness in my own feelings.

This I ask in the name of him who saved me
for all that is beautiful, true, and loving.

Entertainers

God of joy, we thank you
for capacity to enjoy entertainment,
and for those with the skills to entertain us.
We are grateful for
those at the theatre,
in the concert hall,
in our malls and gardens,
or on TV,
who make us clap, cry,
think deeply, or laugh at ourselves.
Thank you for
clowns, singers, comperes,
actors, jugglers, dancers,
magicians and musicians.

Yet save us, God our Saviour,
from taking them too seriously.
Rescue us from treating the world of entertainment
as more real than the duties and joys of our own daily pilgrimage.
Free us from blind adulation
of art which does not glorify you.
Deliver our society from the sin
of turning entertainers into idols,
and from making their personal lives models for our values and goals.

Give us the grace
to have only one Model and one Lord,
for your love's sake.

Shepherd of Your Sheep

We come together, loving God,
in need of encouragement and correction,
confession, challenge, and assurance.
Give to each of us at least one moment of truth today,
when we may know that we are loved and treasured
by the Good Shepherd who knows his sheep by name.

Great Shepherd of the sheep,
let your peace rest on your world family,
that there may be an end of cruelty, anger, war,
persecution, injustice, exploitation, and alienation,
and the way of love begin to rule among all mankind.

Good Shepherd, we ask you this day
to tend your sick ones,
rest your weary ones,
feed your hungry ones,
soothe your suffering ones,
comfort your grieving ones,
pity your afflicted ones,
and rejoice with your joyful ones.*

In your mercy, deepen the hope of this congregation here gathered,
that the future may be faced in the spirit of Jesus Christ our Lord.

* St Augustine

Itinerant Workers

Most loving God,
you sent among us
an itinerant Preacher of no fixed address,
who by the paradox of grace
has opened up a new and living way
for us to be truly at home.

In his name we pray
for itinerant workers
who live rootless lives
so that we might enjoy life more.

We thank you for:
   roadbuilders and maintenance crews
   who live in grey camps beside our highways;
   teachers, clergy, bankers, railway workers,
   policemen, and others, who spend much of
   their lives without a home of their own;
   truckies who spend so many waking hours
   on the highways, away from home;
   itinerant fruit-pickers moving with the seasons
   from the Derwent Valley to Mildura,
   from Barossa to Coffs Harbour,
   from Nambour to Bundaberg.

We pray for the families of these oft-forgotten folk:
   the young people who spend life in caravan parks,
   constantly changing school and losing friends;
   wives who rarely see their husbands,
   and children for whom their father is like a stranger;
   the marriages which break
   under the strain of infrequent cohabitation;
   the mal-adjusted youngsters who have suffered
   emotional damage through constant insecurity.

Each of these wanderers
has a name which you know,
and a life which you treasure.
In your love, be with them
on their journeys
and support them in their crises:
through Jesus Christ, our way, truth, and life.

Small Country Towns

Country life has many joys, O God,
for which we give you thanks.
But when we drive through some towns,
we know that all is not well.

We pray especially for country towns
which are shrinking in size,
with townfolk demoralized and depressed
as old family businesses close,
and the paint on struggling shops
gets more faded and tatty.

We remember the many people
who have been compelled to move
far away from families to find work,
and the unemployed youth who drift
around the pubs and clubs.

We pray for country folk as
schools shrink,
community organizations peter out,
priests and ministers are withdrawn
to larger towns and parishes,
and medical care is reduced.

God, you treasure the people
of these shrinking towns.
Show them how to adjust
in creative ways.
Richly bless that small group of citizens
who struggle to maintain the essential services
and facilities of their communities.

Father of the Galilean,
Father of us all,
hear our prayers.

Children in Hospital

Loving Lord, you know the joys and fears of little children.
Bless your little ones who are in hospital today:
If they are in pain,
give them the strength to bear it with your help.
If they are afraid,
give them the courage to share it with those who nurse them.
If they are so ill that only parents are allowed to visit,
help them to understand they have not been deserted
by sisters, brothers, or friends.

Gentle Lord, help the doctors and nurses
to be gentle, sensitive, and reassuring.
When painful treatment must be administered,
give your children confidence and trust in those who give it.

Put a sweet soothing prayer in the souls of the youngsters
who are too weak or too young to pray for themselves.
Above all else, help them to know they are never alone.
When family or friends leave and kiss them goodnight,
when the lights are turned low and quietness descends,
let them know for sure that you are at their side,
cradling them in strong warm arms,
soothing their fears and filling them with love and peace.

This is our prayer, through Jesus,
who shared our childhood and knows our pain.

Bushfires

Loving God,
our prayers today are where our hearts and minds
have been during last week:
with the victims of the bushfires.

We pray for those who mourn their dead:

families, neighbours, schoolfriends, workmates.
O God, divine Friend,
be with them in their desperate sorrow.
Comfort their torn hearts
and heal them from nightmare memories.
Let there be joy,
let there be peace,
let there be hope,
let there be love.

We pray for the injured survivors in our hospitals:
Those who are severely burnt or disfigured,
and those suffering ones who may never recover.
Relieve them from pain, and soothe their tortured minds
by your Holy Spirit.
Let there be joy,
let there be peace,
let there be hope,
let there be love.

Gracious Lord, we pray for all who lost their homes:
Comfort them as they grieve the loss
of very special personal possessions,
treasured photos or letters,
gifts, heirlooms, or mementos
which held a host of precious memories.
Let there be joy,
let there be peace,
let there be hope,
let there be love.

We pray for the firemen who mourn dead comrades:
Be with them in their distress.
Bless their dedication and courage,
and stir our society to make sure they are provided
with the best facilities and safety equipment
for their vocation.
Let there be joy,
let there be peace,
let there be hope,
let there be love.

We pray for all those working for the rehabilitation of the victims:
The government, Red Cross, the church,
telephonists, social workers, pastors,
and a host of friends, neighbours, and generous citizens.
Give us the grace to help in ways which will respect human dignity,
speed recovery, and restore hope.
Let there be joy,
let there be peace,
let there be hope,
let there be love.
These prayers we ask through the One
Whose Spirit inspires our compassion, Jesus our Lord.

Forgotten People

God of all who labour
and are heavy laden,
awaken within us gratitude
for all the forgotten people
who work behind the scenes
and receive sparse thanks.

We pray for all
   cooks, cleaners and clerks,
   gardeners, garbage collectors and grave diggers,
   secretaries, street sweepers and sandwich makers,
   bakers, brewers and bee-keepers,
   drycleaners, designers and drovers,
   telephonists, traindrivers and typists.

We give thanks, O Lord,
for their loyalty and skill,
and pray that our community
may become more appreciative
of all who toil in the background
to enhance our daily lives.

This we pray
   in the name of the Lord
   who did not shrink
   from washing the feet
   of his followers.

Part VII

AS YOU LOVE YOURSELF
Be with us, Lord

Today in the City

Lord of all life,
Lord of each hour:
Be with us today.

At tram stop or bus station,
at roundabout or traffic light:
Be with us today.

On freeway or footpath,
on stairway or escalator:
Be with us today.

By assembly line or typewriter,
by kitchen sink or computer:
Be with us today.

In clamour or quietness,
in talk or in sickness:
Be with us today.

Among friends or competitors,
among atheists or believers:
Be with us today.

Lord of the beginning,
Lord of the ending:
Be with us today.

Hallowed be Your Name

Wonderful God,
wise beyond our conceiving,
loving beyond our feeling,
our Father by Christ's revealing:
Hallowed be your name.

Through our speaking and listening,
seeking and finding:
Hallowed be your name.

In our loosing and binding,
choosing and discarding:
Hallowed be your name.

By our caring and crying,
sharing and suffering:
Hallowed be your name.

For your Christ and his story,
your kingdom and glory:
Hallowed be your name.

In Spirit and Truth

Spirit of life,
your touch is pure grace,
more gentle than fingers of light,
more sure than arms of granite.

You caress our being
and awaken in us
a passion for more light,
more truth,
greater love.

You are kneading our spirit
with fingers of love
until faith
is no mere doctrine
but our autobiography.

Long Weekend

Lord of all our days,
today we are not finding it easy
to enter into worship with enthusiasm.
Many of our friends are on holiday,
and the congregation is sparse.
We are even a little envious
of the opportunity many have
for a change from the normal routines.
We feel apathetic,
and are in danger of infecting our worship
with a second-rate approach.

Loving God,
rescue us from apathy and envy.
Open our sluggish souls to your Spirit,
that we may awaken to the wonder
of being in your house on this Lord's Day.
Help us to count your mercies in Christ
rather than our absent friends.
Inspire us again
with the joy of this holy day.

Please bless our absent members.
Whether they are worshipping with another congregation,
or experiencing recreation in other ways,
may the life of the Risen One dwell in them.
Turn their holiday into a holy day.
Refresh us all for the ongoing tasks
and privileges of this new week.

Blessed be your name, O Lord.
To you all praise is due,
today and always.

Turn to Us

Lord our God, in the name of Jesus,
help us to break the hold
that failure and discouragement has upon our hearts:
To you, O Lord, we turn for encouragement;
turn to us and help us.

When our sins oppress us, and our spirits grow faint,
and the gloom of failure settles upon us,
help us to see through the shadows:
To you, O Lord, we turn for light;
turn to us and help us.

When we doubt the goodness of life
because evil and suffering blind us to life's goodness,
give us the grace to rise above despair:
To you, O Lord, we turn for grace;
turn to us and help us.

When we are tempted to suppress our deep longing
for goodness, and to deny our better selves,
re-awaken our souls:
To you, O Lord, we turn for renewal;
turn to us and help us.

When we become immersed in trivial pleasures
and material cares, forgetting you,
may the ordinary things of life
bear witness to your presence and goodness.
To you, O Lord, we turn in trust.
Blessed be your name, Saviour and Friend,
the Beginning and End.

Save Your Children

God, most holy and most compassionate,
save your children from the evil
which lies in wait even for your saints.
God of great mercy, we pray
that you will forgive us for our addiction
to words instead of deeds:
Lord, hear us and help us.

That you will rescue us
from our suspicion toward those
who attend a different church,
speak with a different accent,
or vote for a different political party:
Lord, hear us and help us.

That you will make us alert
to the silences or the cries
of those who are too weak
to defend themselves against injustice:
Lord, hear us and help us.

Please awaken our sensitivity
to those hidden fears
and self-dislike
which may make some people so unlovely:
Lord, hear us and help us.

That we may face up
to whatever embarrassment,
apology, or restitution is needed
to right the wrongs we have committed:
Lord, hear us and help us.

That, by the grace, mercy, and peace
of our Lord Jesus Christ,
you will enable us to say goodbye
to old shame, pessimism, and fear,
and be glad to accept your free forgiveness:
Lord, hear us and help us.

Father of Jesus and our God,
in a world of mistrust and ingratitude,
anxiety and miserliness,
we give you thanks for your abundant generosity
and your loyalty toward us:
through our Saviour Christ Jesus.

Shepherd Us

Most loving God,
you are the Shepherd God
who cares for us with an infinite compassion,
seeking to help even the smallest,
   weakest,
   and lowliest
   in your flock.

Grant to us, we pray,
the readiness to put ourselves
under your direction,
that in our weakness
we may have your divine support,
and in our strength
the wisdom to use our power
in ways that will not hurt others.

So shall we fulfil your purposes
declared in our Shepherd King,
Jesus Christ our Lord.

All who are Heavy Laden

In this era of conflicts
 and mountainous problems,
we know what it is to labour
 and be heavy laden.
You have called us to go out
 into all the world
and immerse all nations
 in the Gospel of divine love.
We have tried, Lord,
 and have become tattered and tired,
 despondent, even a bit cynical.
We, the heavy-laden,
 come to you, Lord,
needing your rest.

As the native hen nests
 in the clumps of tussocks
 at the edge of quiet waters,
so give us a nesting place
 in the quiet places of your kingdom,
that our hope may be renewed
 as your mothering Spirit broods over us,
protecting us through
 every dark night of the soul,
until morning comes again
 and we are renewed —
 as if born again —
to learn from you the holy way
 that leads to life
for all humanity.

Be with Us

Creator of the earth and heavens
Lord of the past, present, and future:
Be with us this day.

God of times and seasons,
of fresh life and growth,
and mellow times of fruitfulness:
Be with us this day.

God of hope and joy,
of the loving heart, the gentle spirit,
and the determined will:
Be with us this day.

God of hope and joy, God of the loving heart,
Father of our Lord Jesus Christ, and our God:
Be with us this day.

Peace of God

When my days become over-busy,
and I get hassled by too many worries:
Sweet Lord, give me your peace.

When my vision begins to fade,
and weariness infiltrates the soul:
Strong Lord, give me your peace.

When, disgusted by my own faithlessness,
I toss on my bed through the night:
Faithful Lord, give me your peace.

When worship becomes a routine,
and prayer has the taste of sawdust:
Renewing Lord, give me your peace.

When my hair turns grey above a wrinkled face,
and my energy is spent before the day is done:
Unfailing Lord, give me your peace.

When I'm retired from work with its joys,
and wonder what it means to grow older:
Nurturing Lord, give me your peace.

When my mind glimpses strange sights,
and my heart ceases to beat:
Deathless Lord, give me your peace.

For Deliverance

God of Jesus and our God,
we are grateful for all who come from east and west,
north and south,
to feast in your Kingdom:
We are thankful for Jesus who calls us together.

We are grateful for the various shades
of people and opinion,
age-groups and experience,
which make your church such a unique family:
We are thankful for Jesus who calls us together.

·   *(Silent Meditation)*

Merciful God,
from bitterness, oppression,
war and terrorism:
Deliver your people, Lord.

From a church-life so broad
that it has no conviction,
and a church-life so narrow
that it has no catholic spirit:
Deliver your people, Lord.

From hunger,
homelessness,
unemployment and injustice:
Deliver your people, Lord.

From corruption in governments,
police forces,
and public service:
Deliver your people, Lord.

From shyness in befriending,
panic in suffering,
loneliness in grieving,
and fear in dying:
Deliver your people, Lord.

That the kingdoms of this world
may be gathered
into your eternal kingdom:
Deliver your people, Lord.

Contemporary Wilderness

Lord of life abundant,
keep your church alert
   to the needs of our fellow-Australians
   who become hurt or lost
   in the wilderness of modern life.

Keep us alert
   to the over-sensitive person,
   who puts on a bold front
   but suffers behind the facade.

Keep us alert
   to the disabled or disfigured person,
   who may be suffering
   behind closed doors.

Keep us alert
   to the overworked person,
   weary and exhausted
   in body, mind, and spirit.

Keep us alert
   to the unemployed person
   who is feeling useless,
   rejected, frustrated, and angry.

Keep us alert
   to the bewildered person
   who is 'bushed' by life
   and needs encouragement and guidance.

Keep us alert
   to those facing difficult decisions,
   confronting serious surgery,
   or bearing heavy burdens.

Lord of the wilderness,
keep us alert also
to our own deep needs.
When our path becomes rough
or our thirst begins to burn,
give us not what we ask,
but what we truly need:
through Christ Jesus, our Lord.

Light

God of light,
let your light draw us nearer to you,
and to our neighbours in all the earth,
now and in generations to come —

Nearer to your generosity,
   and to all our hungry and homeless neighbours.
Nearer to your compassion,
   and to those who are broken in body, mind, and spirit.
Nearer to your righteous anger,
   and to people who suffer from mental or physical abuse.
Nearer to your comfort,
   and to those who sorrow because of death or alienation.
Nearer to your all-inclusive love,
   and closer to neighbours who have no faith or hope.
Nearer to your peace,
   and to all who are caught in destructive conflicts.

God of light,
continue to impregnate this grey and bewildered world
with your light,
that the glory of your final purpose
may find a joyous completion in us:
through Jesus Christ our Lord.

Renew Our Spirit

Deep is your love for us, O God.
Great is your compassion;
You have breathed a new spirit into us,
and your Spirit sustains it.

As long as I have breath,
I dedicate my being to you,
my skills and my gifts,
my joy and my love.

But I have failed to fulfil
my rich destiny as your Spirit's child.
I am not living or reflecting
the fulfilled life of Christ Jesus.

My failures are many,
my faults are obvious;
my faith falters,
and my love lapses.

Yet it is still my joy
to accept your forgiveness in Christ Jesus,
to bear witness to your love,
and to cling to your vision
of a new heaven and a new earth.

God most wonderful,
we place our longings for a nobler life before you,
and look to your abundant mercy:
through Jesus Christ our Lord.

Part VIII

FOR SHEPHERDS ONLY
Ministers, Pastors and Priests

New in the Parish

Living God,
thank you for the privileges
of being an ordained pastor
within your church.

For the honour of expounding
the Holy Bible
and the joy of celebrating Holy Communion:
I give you my gratitude.

For the favour and responsibility
of speaking your word of forgiveness
to broken spirits:
I give you my gratitude.

For the welcome
I receive as I move into a new parish,
and the respect, love, and trust so freely given:
I give you my gratitude.

For the pleasure
of invitations into homes,
and the fun of sharing a family meal:
I give you my gratitude.

For being allowed
to assist people
in their time of need:
I give you my gratitude.

For the wonder of witnessing
bushed and defeated folk
rediscover their faith and confidence:
I give you my gratitude.

For being supported
by those whom we support,
and blessed by those whom we bless:
I give you my gratitude.

I thank you for my calling,
and praise you for the grace
of my Lord, Jesus Christ.

Serving at Table

God most holy,
your love is awesome.

As I stand before
this holy Table,
I wish you had a celebrant
worthy to be here.

I am not worthy
to gather up the crumbs
from under your table,
but you have invited me
like an honoured guest.

That I should be your servant
in this Mystery,
causes me to tremble
with that unique fear
composed of awe and love.

May I discern
the presence of the Body
as I eat and drink of things divine,
lest, victim of familiarity,
I miss the Host,
though touching the gift.

Our Peculiar Temptations

God, you search me and know me;
save me from the peculiar temptations
to which a minister is exposed.

From allowing holy words and tasks
to become mere rite and habit:
Deliver me, O God.

From the lust for self-display
which feeds on public appearance:
Deliver me, O God.

From that bogus humility
which craves the reputation of being humble:
Deliver me, O God.

From allowing the expectations of parishioners
to shape haphazardly my attitudes and priorities:
Deliver me, O God.

From the unwillingness to recognize and use
the diverse skills of lay people:
Deliver me, O God.

From offloading to the laity
only those tasks I find distasteful:
Deliver me, O God.

From being unwilling to seek counsel
from other clergy or laity:
Deliver me, O God.

From the insecurity which makes me jealous
when other ministers seem more competent than I:
Deliver me, O God.

Lord of the Church,
give me the grace
to love these people
with whom I minister,
and to allow them
to love me.

Enigma

God, the name above all other names,
sometimes I think my name is Enigma:
Made in your image,
but sculptured from dirt;
Possessing your breath,
   but inhaling with infected lungs;
Owning Jesus as my true Brother,
   but also related to Judas and Pilate;
As clear as moonlight over frosty paddocks,
   but as muddy as a buffalo's wallow.

Yet, on my best days,
when the air is clear
   and the sun is shining,
my spirit hovers like a lark
   between earth and sky,
singing the loveliest melodies
   I have learnt on earth,
longing, longing to unite them
   with the music of the heavens.

O God, because you truly love
this human enigma,
and made me a member
of your family,
let me learn some notes
   with which angels praise you,
and grant me the grace to echo them
   amid the mundane stuff of life.
For your love's sake.

Bitter Cup

Today, Lord, I saw a mother take
her dying child
   from the hospital cot
   and enfold him in her arms.
   She mopped the little fevered face
   and when dry lips
   whispered 'Mummy'
   I saw a woman
   writhe in anguish
   unspeakable.

Today, Lord, I saw a father hold
his dead child
   in his arms
   and watched him
   place the little body
   back at last
   in the barren cot
   soundlessly,
   in the agony
   of raw grief.

Lord, I felt so wordless,
overwhelmed with grief
   for the grieving.
   The one true thing
   for me to do
   was to put arms around them
   and whisper the Word
   about a holy cross
   where you
   tasted the bitter cup,
   then lead them away
   from the ward.

Lord, at times
it is only that Word
which stands between
me and the nightmare
of utter despair.

One Minute before the Sermon

Holy God,
at this moment I am a little
awed and scared
just as I have been
a thousand times before.
I want this sermon to be
a holy experience
for these people and for me.

Yet I know
that my motives are mixed.
There is within me
one overwhelming desire
that as the preacher
I may be a nobody:
that the Gospel may be heard
and not the preacher.

But also in me
is another want:
to be a successful preacher,
just as at other times
I want to be
a successful pastor.

Please take
my mixed abilities and motives,
the love I have for you
and the love I have for myself,
and let them be welded
into one strong unity
by the fire of your Spirit.
Let the living Word
be heard,
through me,
or in spite of me.
Let all be to your glory!

PHOTO CREDITS

Cover Banksia prionotes, WA (I. Traeger)

Page
- 8 Pioneer farmhouse ruins, SA (P. Furnell)
- 13 Shearing the rams (J. Pohl)
- 18 River reflections (B. Grieger)
- 33 Riding the waves (G. Smith)
- 34 Standley Chasm at noon, NT (J. Hoopmann)
- 37 Surging flood-waters (J. Pohl)
- 49 Battered, but strong (J. Hoopmann)
- 53 St John's Church spire, Barossa Valley, SA
- 57 Sunrise (J. Sawade)
- 60 Billabong, west of Alice Springs, NT (I. Traeger)
- 65 Boats at dawn, Granite Island, SA (J. Pohl)
- 67 Toadstools (J. Pohl)
- 68 Wild flower, Badgindarra (J. Hoopmann)
- 72 Windmill (J. Pohl)
- 75 Cricket crowd (G. Smith)
- 77 Pelican, Coorong, SA (G. Smith)
- 85 Eucalypts, Central Australia (J. Gregor)
- 89 Sunset, Flinders Ranges, SA (L. Doubtfire)
- 91 Strolling in the park (G. Smith)
- 94 Fishing at Waitpinga, SA (J. Pohl)
- 96 Green glory (G. Smith)
- 104 Festival Theatre, Adelaide (Adelaide City Council)
- 109 Rundle Mall, Adelaide (Adelaide City Council)
- 113 Kangaroo and friends, Cleland Park, SA (J. Pohl)
- 115 Sturt pea, Flinders Ranges, SA (L. Doubtfire)
- 123 Aboriginal, Hermannsburg, NT (I. Traeger)
- 127 Aboriginal rock paintings, NT (B. Grieger)
- 135 Bushfire havoc, 1983 (J. Gregor)
- 141 Holiday peace (J. Pohl)
- 143 Reverie in the dusk (G. Smith)
- 147 Anthill near Pine Creek, NT (J. Hoopmann)